FOOLS RUSH IN

By Vaughn Phelps

V. I. P.
PUBLISHING

First publication 2014 By Vaughn Phelps
All rights reserved. No parts of this book may be reproduced, stored in a retrieval system or transmitted in any form or by any means without the express, written permission of the Publisher, except by a reviewer who may quote brief passages to be used by a newspaper, magazine, anthology or journal.

This book is a collection of fiction. Names, places and incidents are the creation of the author's imagination and are used in a fictional content. Any resemblance to persons living or dead is purely coincidental.

COPYRIGHT 2014
ISBN #978-0-9838938-6-8
Published in America by V. I. P.
P.O. Box # 911
Twin Falls, Idaho 83303-911

ACKNOWLEDGEMENTS

Cover design: Mitzi Michelle Phelps
Cover model: Megan Elaine Phelps
Editing: Ginny Greene.

FOREWORD

I don't believe in giving too much away and I hate synopses. I think it's like conducting an autopsy while the patient is still alive and struggling to get off the table. An introduction is like seeing the bride without her make-up, her hair still in curlers and her wedding dress hanging in the closet.

FOOLS RUSH IN
TABLE OF CONTENTS

CHAPTER-1 PLAYBOYS CAN BE CAUGHT IF YOU USE THE RIGHT BAIT
CHAPTER-2 EVERYBODY MEETS AT KIRK'S PLACE
CHAPTER-3 NOT SINGING IN THE RAIN
CHAPTER-4 WATER PLEASURE
CHAPTER-5 FARMER'S MARKET, WITH NO FARMERS
CHAPTER-6 LIKE CLOCKWORK
CHAPTER-7 RECENT HISTORY
CHAPTER-8 ANY PUBLICITY IS GOOD PUBLICITY?
CHAPTER-9 WHAT'S IN YOUR WALLET?
CHAPTER-10 BURGLARY, THEFT AND BUNCO AS A HOBBY
CHAPTER-11 STYXX AND STONES
CHAPTER-12 WILDLIFE IN THE BIG CITY
CHAPTER-13 NATURAL-LY
CHAPTER-14 STYXX AHOY
CHAPTER-15 PARKHURST FROM THE OUTSIDE
CHAPTER-16 BACK AT…WELL, IF YOU'VE BEEN PAYING ATTENTION, YOU KNOW
CHAPTER-17 COUNTING COUP
CHAPTER-18 NOW AREN'T YOU GLAD YOU READ THIS FAR?
CHAPTER-19 WHO'S ON FIRST?
CHAPTER-20 OH, IT HURTS SO BAD
CHAPTER-21 DONUT BASE CAMP
CHAPTER-22 EXPRESS YOURSELF

CHAPTER-23 THEY DON'T PLAY POLO AT NIGHT
CHAPTER-24 SAM SPADE HAD TO DO HIS OWN LEG WORK
CHAPTER-25 EXECUTIVE TERMINALS ARE MORE PLEASANT
CHAPTER-26 OVERLOOKING CENTRAL PARK
CHAPTER-27 MUSIC APPRECIATION
CHAPTER-28 PARKS AREN'T JUST FOR KIDS AND DOGS

FOOLS RUSH IN

STORY BASED ON THE ORIGINAL SCREENPLAY OF THE SAME NAME
By Vaughn Phelps

CHAPTER-1
PLAYBOYS CAN BE CAUGHT IF YOU USE THE RIGHT BAIT

In the approaching dusk, Melanie bends toward the streetlight. The cold, near tornado winds billow her coat and almost drive her back onto the sidewalk. She looks up at the street sign, leans into the weather and crosses the street toward a large, impressive brownstone high-rise, The Parkhurst. Just as she reaches the entryway, a black Lincoln Continental rounds the corner and parks. Rain starts with a vengeance.

Kirk, early thirties, ruggedly handsome, wearing only a towel, hangs a tux on his closet door, spreads canned chicken onto a saucer beside a small pet door. With eight bars of,

"AIN'T MISBEHAVIN',"

an electronic Fats Waller announces a visitor. Kirk views a closed circuit TV, shuts down a coded alarm system, takes the telegram. From a carved jade bowl on the teak and ivory table by the door he gives the Western Union messenger a handful of quarters. Relocking the three-inch door, he opens the missive.

> Kirk Cannard, Parkhurst #702, Manhattan, N.Y.
> Kirk, tonight would be a mistake STOP
> You don't want a serious relationship STOP
> Go to the ball without me STOP
> You might meet someone there who can live without a
> long-term commitment STOP
> Karen

Kirk punches a number into his speed dial, "I don't think I can make it. Something's come up."

A filtered voice answers, "As captain of last year's winning polo team, you <u>must</u> present this year's trophy."

"Let me get back to you. I was just about to cancel Bergdorf Goodman."

Melanie slips through the triple-locked door into the secure entryway behind a tall, rain-coated man and Pekingese in matching outfits. Under the closed circuit camera she pauses, seems to study the electronic security code-numbered system. She catches the inner door as an elderly woman with half-inch thick make-up exits. Taking the elevator to nine, she walks down two floors and pushes the button at #702. She hears,

"AIN'T MISBEHAVIN'."

Kirk opens and, almost bowled over by her explosive entrance, he grabs the towel as it starts to slip.

"I thought you were going to let me freeze my ass off out there." She drips, removes her coat and shakes rainwater from it. It sets up an internal rippling effect. In the expensive knit dress and matching boots, the body is truly a masterpiece of the sculptor's art.

Kirk shows more than a passing interest in the motion. "That would be a terrible shame."

"I walked three blocks from where I left the taxi. I'm still trying to catch my breath."

"So I see."

"I'm not here for small talk. Let's get down to business."

"Sure! What business is that?"

"My God, I'm catching pneumonia and I'm stuck with a little boy who wants to play grown-up."

"I don't know that you're stuck at all. The door works both ways."

"Will you get on with it? Damn, I'll never again go through this with some unknown."

"I'd love to play twenty questions, but I'm about to shave."

"Money. Do I have to spell it out in words of one syllable?"

He starts for the bathroom. She follows, pulls a small .25 and aims at him. He turns quickly, twists the gun from her hand and throws it onto the bed.

"Money's two syllables, but you've made a mistake...." He pulls her driver's license from her alligator shoulder bag and reads, "...Melanie."

He answers the ringing phone with a robot-like voice. "Kirk can't come to the phone, but if you'll leave your message at the sound of..." PAUSE. "Come over, Lucinda, I'll make you some herbal tea." PAUSE. "Okay, rest. Come when you're well." PAUSE. "No,

I've fed Kiva. She can get along without you for a day."
He hangs up, shaves and watches Melanie in the mirror. "My housekeeper found a new illness unnamed by medical science, so naturally she had to have it."

She picks up the handgun. "Now look—"

"No, you look. I paid sixteen thousand for that vase from Catherine the Great's summer palace. The piano was purchased after a Van Cliburn concert for seventy-two thousand. I don't play or read music. The Persian rug I purchased when the U.S Embassy pulled out of Iran. The broker carried it out over his shoulder under machine gun fire." He moves to an ornate marble bar, holds up a silver-topped, cut glass decanter. "This bar is from a Medici castle. I only drink brandy on special occasions."

"What's that to me? You've got my money."

"I'm just pointing out that if I wanted whatever it is you're after, I'd have it. And your little popgun wouldn't stop me." He looks her over again, from head to toe. "In fact, if I wanted you, I'd have you." He finishes shaving, drops the towel and enters the shower. Looking confused, she waits, holds up an oversized towel as he steps out and dries off.

"You really don't have my money?"

He gives her an even more appraising look. "How much do you... No, scratch that. Another time I might be tempted, but if you'll forget business for one evening, I'll be dressed and..."

"Oh! You've gotten the wrong impression. You think I'm a hooker."

"...we'll have dinner and talk."

"If you don't have my money, why should I?"

"Because I've decided I will have you."

"I think not." She edges toward the door.

"That door is Hawaiian Koa wood sandwiched between bulletproof steel. The tamper-proof lock opens only by code. If you try to force it, the charge starts at only 10,000 volts, but it builds quickly."

She turns flashing dark eyes on him. "What do you want? If you know nothing about this, what are you after?"

"I told you. I'm interested. I'll help you find your money."

She goes to the window, pulls back the curtain and sees a black Lincoln Continental and one man, Long Cigar, behind the wheel and Hearing Aid beside him in the front seat. She says nothing, but suddenly tenses and her hand grips the curtain.

Kirk phones. "We'll be a little late. My date still has to change."

Without looking away from the window, she says, over her shoulder, "I don't know what sophomoric game you're playing, but count me out."

He dials another number.

"This is Mr. Cannard, can you change the sizes? Dark, 5'2", 100 pounds, size two-three, shoes, three?" PAUSE. "I think so, something appropriate. How long?" PAUSE. "Thank you, I much appreciate it."

The Continental is still there. She looks away from the window long enough to glare at him and lets the curtain fall."

"You're crazy if you think I'm going anywhere with you."

"We'll discuss it in the car, but you'd better take a quick shower. You look like a drowned rat."

"What's this event you're going to?"

"<u>We're</u> going to an awards banquet."

"If I agree, I can leave when it's over?"

"Do I look like someone who has to use force to get a woman?"
"Well, that's what you're doing."
"I think you need a friend."
"Sure."
"And a good meal."

The rain beats a staccato drumming on the Continental's roof. From the fogged windshield and black leather interior, the two men watch the Parkhurst's entrance. Long Cigar exhales a cloud of blue smoke. "I tell 'ya we're too late. We musta' missed her."
"What?"
"Turn that thing up."
"What?"
"Why buy the damn thing if you never turn it up?"
"Wait a minute. I'll turn this up. Then I can hear you. Now, what'ja say?"
"We're too late; we shouldn'ta took that turn at 5th."
"Let's go in an' check."
"Nah, let's wait, get her when she comes out."
"Okay. I'll go in. You stay here an' watch, case she comes out. Gimme your piece, I din't bring mine."
"Carry it from now on. What the hell am I, Nationwide Rent-a-Gun?"
Taking a .45 from under his arm, Long Cigar cocks it, puts it on safety and gives it to Hearing Aid, who crosses the street, turns off his hearing aid and waits for an opportunity to enter. Long Cigar slumps, puffs and fills the car's interior with dark, oily smoke.

CHAPTER-2
EVERYBODY MEETS AT KIRK'S PLACE

Wearing nothing but a towel, Melanie looks about to bolt. He puts his hand on the back of her neck, pulls her forward and kisses her. Even with the bedroom window open just a crack, lightning has left the scent of ozone and electricity wafting in the air, although, the electricity might not be from the lightning alone.

With,

"AIN'T MISBEHAVIN',"

Kirk answers the door and admits a man and woman pulling several wheeled steamer trunks labeled B-G on the side. Melanie, in black bra, panties and hose, stuffs the .25 into her purse and watches in amazement as an assortment of expensive gowns are held up in front of her. The woman dresses her as the man sweeps her hair into a sculpted miracle, then does her make-up. At the last minute, the woman takes her shoulder bag, transfers hankie and lipstick to a satin purse. There's no time to retrieve her gun as Kirk pulls a stunningly glamorous Melanie to the door.

Moments later, the limo driver holds an umbrella over them while they climb in. Kirk turns and gives the umbrella to a passing, bedraggled bag lady. As Melanie is taking her seat, she looks anxiously across the street. The black Continental is still in place, but the interior is so filled with thick fog of cigar smoke, no one inside could see out.

Only steps behind, Hearing Aid pads down the thick-carpeted stairs. He enters the lobby from the second floor. With his hearing Aid turned on, he might have heard them leaving the foyer, less than ten feet away.

A wide banner proclaims the "B.O.N.K. Award Dinner" in the Ritz Ballroom; an up-scale event is well into the program. The dinner dishes have been cleared away, but Kirk, dragging a reluctant Melanie, is cheered, glad-handed and backslapped as he makes his way to the speaker's table. He holds her hand tightly, preventing her from slipping away.

"You never said you were some damn celebrity." She scavenges unclaimed chocolate desserts from those seated at the speaker's table, slips to a nearby table, capturing several more. As Kirk finishes his speech and awards the trophy to the new recipient, the waiter whispers that he's seen Melanie stuffing a linen napkin into her purse.

Out of view of others, Kirk, smiling, pries the purse from her fingers and removes the napkin. A diamond necklace falls into his hand.

"This is Mrs. Faulkner's. I thought you were just stealing hotel silverware." He pulls her back into her seat then moves to a nearby table. He bends behind a dowager. "You haven't missed this yet, Margarete. My companion found it on the floor, but didn't know its owner. Luckily I recognized it."

He hooks the necklace around the woman's neck and returns to the speaker's table.

Melanie keeps her head down. "I was just..."
"Yeah, I know."
"You know nothing."
"We'll talk about it at home."

"You said…"

"That was before I knew you were going to steal from my friends."

"I didn't."

"You tried. But maybe you'd rather tell your story to the police. They're all around."

"What?"

"Special security, off duty police working as waiters."

"We'll…talk at home."

CHAPTER-3
NOT SINGING IN THE RAIN

Water dripping from the end of his nose and water-filled shoes sloshing, Hearing Aid climbs into the Continental. "There's no way she could'a got out the back."

"Well, she din' come out the front so we gonna have ta wait."

"Nah, I say one's better than none." He throws the .45 on the seat. "We'll get her later."

Long Cigar pulls the car into a water-splashing U turn.

* * * * * *

A bronze French Empire clock STRIKES as Kirk locks the apartment door behind them. Melanie shows him her soaked paper with the address. "I was to meet my brother here. He must have gotten the address wrong."

"Don't make a mistake into a catastrophe. You were looking for someone, but it wasn't any brother."

"I don't know what you mean."

"Tonight's fundraiser was the B.O.N.K. group, The Brotherhood Of Needy Kids. You asked me what KNOB stood for. I thought at first you were kidding, but then I realized that you suffer from dyslexia."

Her rapid intake belies her disclaimer. "No! I...I overcame it when I was a child."

"You <u>think</u> you overcame it."

"Well, sometimes, when I'm excited..."

"You wanted apartment 207. This is 702."

17

"Damn!"

"Probably the luckiest mistake you'll ever make."

"What do you mean?"

"Tell me the truth."

"I can't."

Frantically, she looks around, notes the expensive ivory figurines, the pre-Columbian artifacts, and certificates from Greenpeace, Friends of the Earth, S.P.C.A. Fellowship, JUNTO Membership and Zoological Society Docent.

"There were men following me. I don't know what they wanted, but they're gone now so I can leave."

"I think not."

She quivers and her deep breathing puts a strain on the tight traditional "little black dress' spaghetti straps.

"You mean you'll let me go in the morning, after you've had your way with me?"

He shakes his head and frowns at her. "You're hung up on sex. Frankly, although you're not exactly repulsive, you're certainly not my type and you're too skinny."

"Sure, that's why the guest speaker has to use extortion to get a date."

"I'm going down to talk to your friend in 207, the one who has your money."

"No! Don't! Please…don't."

"You'll have to come along. I can't trust you here alone. You'd have the place stripped before I got back."

"Speaking of sexual hang-ups, I couldn't miss those double entendres."

"Let's go."

"Let me change first."

"You won't need a B & E outfit. We're going to knock at the door, not break in."

"The dress from BG's."

"Oh, right."

"And after you see how harmless everything is, I can just leave from there."

"Yeah, sure."

She starts to put on her still-damp dress, changes her mind and just pulls the trench coat over lacy black bra and panties, then hangs her dress over the towel rack to finish drying.

Moments later, Kirk knocks at #207, but gets no answer. Melanie takes something from her purse and uses it to pick the lock. They enter and see a wide pool of blood surrounding a man face down on the hardwood floor. Kirk feels for a pulse, finds none. As she starts to scream, he grabs her and covers her mouth with a kiss. She struggles, but at the same time, he presses her carotid artery until she passes out. He looks quickly, but finds no gun. Using a fireman's carry, he picks her up and heads toward the elevator. The elderly couple at #205 peeks out their door.

Kirk smiles, "Anniversary. She forgot how champagne sneaks up on her."

The couple nods knowingly.

Carefully sliding Melanie onto his bed, he pours brandy from the silver-topped, cut-glass decanter into a snifter and holds it to her lips. She chokes, coughs, swallows and tries to sit up.

Kirk says, "'Where am I' is cliché. Be original, say..."

She blinks her eyes open and says, "Where am I?"

"You're on a gondola. We're escaping Interpol through the canals of Venice. You've just stolen the

19

Machiavellian aphrodisiac formula that will make me your sex slave."

"Now I remember. I'm with a crazy man who kidnapped me and is holding me against my will."

"Wrong, I'm the sucker who gave you a chance to steal. You're dressed like Cinderella. Look, you've lost your slipper. That means I'm your Prince Charming."

"I'm missing both shoes. No telling what else. It proves you're a sex pervert, a rapist, a degenerate..." *But, some kinda kisser.*

>He holds up one black suede shoe, size three.
>
>"Some chance. But it wasn't like that. The necklace was just a...a target of opportunity."
>
>"The law sees it as taking property belonging to another."
>
>"I was desperate. I had no money, friends or family, no place to go."
>
>"I'll have to call the police."
>
>"But we gave back the necklace."
>
>"I mean about the dead body."
>
>"NO! You mustn't. They'd ask if we knew the man."
>
>"Did we?"
>
>"I think I know who he might be."
>
>"Tell me."
>
>"Not here. Take me away. Promise not to call the police and I'll tell you everything."
>
>"I can't promise that. You might attack me and ravage me."
>
>"And you'd turn me in for that?"
>
>"Now that you mention it, no. Okay, until I hear your whole story, I promise."
>
>"Good, let's go."

"I'll get some blankets."

"Look, you're not the ugliest guy I've ever met. Maybe after we've known each..."

"See, you're the one with a one-track mind. The blankets are for the boat. I don't keep linen aboard. It gets musty."

"'Course, I knew that!"

CHAPTER-4
WATER PLEASURE

"STYXX" is the largest sloop at the dock. Long Cigar and Hearing Aid leave the black Continental and climb aboard.

MUMBLED voices come from below deck, then SHOUTING. Moments later, Long Cigar and Hearing Aid return to the Continental. Dejectedly, they drive off.

* * * * * * *

Coming from his bedroom, Kirk finds Melanie ransacking his kitchen cupboards for food. Kirk is resplendent in expensive persimmon slacks and white polo shirt. Her eyes bug out. "Jeez, wear a neon sign why don'tcha?"

With a look of complete superiority, he says, "I have nothing to hide." He phones for a taxi.

"What's with the cab?"

"Did you drive?"

"No."

"It's only about three miles. Wanna walk?"

"You're even crazier than I thought."

"I don't own a car."

"A sport like you? With all your money?"

"It's too much trouble, besides, I don't like to drive. You can't see all the neat places you've been."

"Super."

"Plus, we can't be traced by the license plates."

"Great."

"Also, nobody can tie on a bomb."

"What?"

"Just bringing the conversation down to something to which you'd relate."

"Fantastic. Can we go now?"

"Hold out your arms."

He piles blankets, sheets and pillows on her, hangs her alligator purse around her neck. He pins a twenty-dollar bill and a note to the kitchen bulletin board. Melanie has time only to grab the decanter of brandy and glance at his note. It's appended to a magazine tear sheet with Kirk's photo and name over an article entitled "Collecting Valuable Ivory." He guides her gently toward the front door, carrying only a silver and ivory handled umbrella. "Okay, I have my load; you have yours. We're away."

She nods her head toward his note on the bulletin board. "Was that note about me?"

"I said I wouldn't be available for lunch with my ex mother-in-law." He sets a code into the lock and pushes her out the door. She can't see over the pile of bedding. Out in the steady rain, he holds the cab door open for her.

"How gallant."

"Anything for Jenny Valentine." To the cab driver, he says, "Citibank on fifty-ninth."

"I thought you said—"

"I have to stop and get some cash."

"You have no money? After all that big talk?"

"I usually go places where I'm known and I don't need cash."

"Sensational."

Moments later, at the ATM, he leaves the cab door open while he gets cash from the machine. A tattered bum rattles a tin cup at him. He drops a twenty in the cup. The bum stares at it open-mouthed. Climbing back into the cab, he says to the driver, "The all night market on Broadway."

"Now what?"

"There's no food aboard. We need to pick up groceries."

"Stupendous."

* * * * * *

The cab pulls away as a police car parks and two uniformed enter the building. They wait as the Parkhurst manager unlocks the door and allows them into #207. "I'm sure the gunshot came from in here, officers."

As soon as they're inside the stuffy apartment, they see the body and call for homicide and the Black Mariah.

CHAPTER-5
FARMER'S MARKET, WITH NO FARMERS

The cab parks in the Farmer's Market loading zone. With the back door open, the driver turns and sees the flap of Melanie's coat blown open. Above the boots, shapely legs and skimpy black lace panties are enticingly revealed. Kirk reaches over and pulls the flap closed. To the cab driver he says, "I won't be long. If the lady gets antsy and wants you to take her someplace, be advised, she has no money and you'd probably be missing the seat cushions when she's gone."

"Are you kiddin' me? I wouldn't miss the rest o' this for nothin'." He adjusts the rear view mirror to see only Melanie.

A short time later, Kirk loads three heaped bags of groceries onto the seat beside Melanie. Seeing a large dog with ribs showing, sniffing an empty burger wrapper, he returns to the market. Minutes later, he spreads several Moist-n-Meaty packets for the dog. Melanie is eating a banana and making her next selection from the brown paper bag buffet. Her mouth filled with potato chips, she says, "You forgot chocolates."

"I have Bakers cocoa on board."

"Oh, be still my heart."

It's a short ride through clear, crisp air. Birds are singing. Temporarily, the rain has stopped and left everything clean and sparkling.

Adjacent to the Empire State Yacht Basin, Kirk unlocks a gate to the Fair Winds Yacht Club. Melanie sees Kirk's name over a berth with a sloop named "Fore

Play." "I might have known you'd choose a name like that."

"Wrong. That belongs to a friend from Newport News. Mine is having a new radar system installed."

He leads her to the end of the dock, where the ketch, "Night Song," is tied to the Knickerbocker Marine Electronics berth. Once aboard, Kirk puts his essential groceries—bacon, eggs, hash browns, limes, tequila, smoked oysters, peanut butter, avocados and sour cream—away. He starts the stove and prepares breakfast. On her own, Melanie searches everything below deck. When she finds nothing of value to help with her occupation, she spreads blankets and pillows over the main stateroom's king-size bed.

"I'm fixing bacon and eggs. You look starved."

"Umm, haven't eaten since yesterday."

"You're Harikrishna and you went too long with your fast?"

"No. See, I had this date with a guy who promised to feed me at a fancy-shmancy banquet. But like all men, he was just another flake." She looks into the head. "Does the water work?"

"Should. I'm on city water and power."

"Good, I need a hot shower."

"Want company?"

"Later, maybe."

"Okay. I'll be in here cookin'."

"Can't really start cookin' without me."

Over a lumberjack's meal, Melanie, barefoot, wrapped in a towel, with no make-up and hair still damp, asks, "Who's Kiva?"

"Who, indeed. She's a Central Park raccoon we found months ago going through our garbage. She had three cubs and like you, looked half starved. We fed her and now, nightly, she expects the same."

"WE?"

"Well, my housekeeper, Lucinda, normally feeds her, but I made the pet door so she could come and go as she pleases."

* * * * * *

Police move about the crime scene in a casual search. They do it carefully, without disturbing the chalk outline of a body. Another uniformed officer enters, carrying a single black suede woman's shoe, size three.

"Captain, I found this in the hall."

CHAPTER-6
LIKE CLOCKWORK

With dawn only minutes away, the eastern sky is a Crayola box of color. Kirk piles dirty dishes in the sink and says, "Some mornings, up on deck, you can see the beginning of time on the horizon."

With chocolate on her lips, Melanie is stretched atop the bed, still wrapped in the towel. She holds a huge Hershey bar. With the wind-whipped water and the vessel rocking gently from side to side, she looks like a baby in a cradle, but is shaped like no baby you ever saw. "I found this in the kitchen."

"The galley."

"Whatever."

He leans over her, pulls the dockside curtain closed. Her arms go around him and pull him down on top of her. She kisses him gently, then again, and he settles beside her. His mouth, also, is now chocolate covered. He licks his lips, and then does the same for her. Except for the towel, she's wearing only a white metal necklace that spells out "Spoiled Rotten."

"What's this?"

"A tongue-in-cheek birthday gift from my father. He said if I was ever desperate, I could pawn it for a couple of thousand. It's platinum."

"But the message…?"

"That's the double-edge part. He meant it."

"And he was probably right?"

"No question."

Later, in the dark, Kirk's voice interrupts the soft gurgle of waves lapping at the sides of the ship. "I must admit, you have a fascinating way of stalling."

"Look, it's been fun, but I should warn you not to expect anything lasting."

"Okay. Tell me what happened last night."

"I mean, you're attractive and interesting, but I'm not looking for a long term relationship."

"I understand. Now tell me what happened."

"It's nothing. It's just...something related to my job."

"Yeah, cut the con job."

"Really. Anyway, with all we've been through together, you should allow a poor girl to keep a few innocent secrets"

"One more chance, then we go to the police."

"If I tell you, then you'll help me?"

"Let's just say I won't turn you in until I know more."

"That's not much of a promise."

With a sliver of overcast daylight entering the cabin, he says nothing, just stares into her dark eyes.

She sighs deeply. "Okay. You won't feel so friendly after you've heard my story, but I think I'm in a little over my head."

"Then tell me. Fast."

"I'm an horologist from Boston. Like my grandfather and his before him, my father was a watchmaker. They all had lifelong careers with Waltham. I'd also planned on that, but when mechanical watches and clocks became expendable commodities, I had to find a new career."

"Spy?"

"No."

"Locksmith?"

"Close."

"How close?"

"I'll just give you the short version. It was last night, 5:30 P.M., in the Havilland Museum."

He sits up and turns on the small overhead reading light. "Wait a minute. Sundays they close at four."

"Whose story is this?" She pulls him back down, kisses him and turns out the light.

CHAPTER-7
RECENT HISTORY

FLASHBACK

At the Havilland Museum, a black-clad feminine figure climbs down from a ceiling panel above the ladies toilet stall. Keeping to the shadows, Melanie, in a form-fitting black jump suit and multiple thick stockings over her running shoes, pulls a black ski mask over her face. With bungee cords over her arm, she listens, then silently climbs a staircase. From the balcony, she looks down onto the Smithsonian rare and unique American coin display.

She fastens the bungee chords and swings down to within easy reach. One by one, she removes only a small number of pre-selected coins, placing them into a fitted case and replacing them with counterfeits. The real coins are displayed obverse side up. She replaces the phonies the same way, but she puts the real coins into her own case, reverse side up.

FLASHFORWARD

Kirk leans on an elbow and turns the light back on. "Wait a minute. I heard about that on the six o'clock news. But they caught the thief before he got out of the building. All the coins were recovered."
She turns out the light. "That's...what THEY think."

He turns on the light. "What about the guy in #207?"

She knocks his elbow out, and he drops onto the pillow. She turns off the light and in the dark, there are more sounds of kissing.

Hours later, she interrupts her jumping jack calisthenics to throw a pillow at the lump in bed. "Hey! You gonna sleep all day?"

"I never rise before noon. It's uncivilized."

"That poetic business about dawn is when you get to bed? You party every night?"

"Not every night, but there's no point living in Manhattan and letting life pass you by. No point living anywhere and not enjoying it."

"When do you work?"

"I'm always working."

"Sure. You don't exercise either?"

"I believe in low-impact aerobics."

"You mean like last night? The horizontal Samba?" She hastily puts something in her mouth and holds up a silver-framed photo.

"What's that? You found more candy?"

"No. Who's this? You have her picture all over the boat."

"That's my ex-wife and it's called a ship or vessel, not a boat."

"Whatever. Most men would only keep an ex's picture to throw knives at."

"I'm not most men. What's in your hand?"

"Nothing."

"Now we're not going through this again."

"It's not important."

"I'll decide that."

He opens her hand and sees a rainbow collection of pills.

"The big yellow ones are diet pills."

"Why?"

"I have a weight problem."

"You're kidding. Even shoving chocolate in your face all day, what are you, a hundred pounds soaking wet?"

"I'd be a blimp without them. I weighed a hundred and eleven last summer."

"What about the green pills?

"They're..."

"Uppers?

"No, downers. You have to understand I was really stressed out last night."

"How about the blue ones?"

"Those are the uppers." She skips into the galley and makes a smoked oyster and banana sandwich. When she offers to make him one, he almost gags.

Kirk takes his cell phone up on deck and calls. "Ethan, I'm interested in the museum heist. I want everything A.S.A.P. Not just headlines, but in-depth stuff that the police don't want to get out. Send the electronic data to the apartment and bring me a hard copy. I'm at the slip."

CHAPTER-8
ANY PUBLICITY IS GOOD PUBLICITY?

At twenty-eight, Ethan looks eighteen and always wears bright red suspenders, sox and bow tie. With "Data Intercept" in gold letters on the glass door, he holds a cell phone and makes notes in red ink.

Cannard Ent. Bill as usual. Police report, museum security, break-ins, losses, carrier's reports, and key personnel.

"This sounds like that girl's volleyball team or the youth choir that you…" PAUSE. "Yes, sir. I understand. I'll get right on it."

* * * * * *

Homicide Lieutenant Pisanti, tall, well-built, with swarthy good looks, moves about in #207. The manager, held back by yellow crime scene tape, tries to see past him into the apartment.

"You say this Charles Blakely rented the apartment for the week?"

"No, Lieutenant. He wanted to spend a week to better appraise his feelings and emotions."

"Can you make that a little plainer for a simple street cop?"

"These units are all privately owned and the lowest price is now nine hundred thousand for a one-bedroom basement unit. He wanted to be sure it was right for him."

"That's…unfurnished?"

"Plus utilities and a twenty-five-hundred-a-month maintenance charge. Garage space is extra."

"And you know nothing else about him?"

"I'd have checked his references if he had decided to take the apartment or a deposit check had bounced."

"He paid by check?"

"No. Cash. Three thousand."

"And he's from Chicago?"

"Lake Pleasant. A small suburb."

"That's all you know? He had no visitors?"

"He'd only been here three days."

"Well, I hope we get something from the prints. So far no one's come forward with any information." The lieutenant ushers him out, locks and seals the door with a special CRIME SCENE padlock.

The manager watches him leave and mumbles to himself. *His bank seemed to know him quite well.*

* * * * * *

News and TV cameras crowd the front steps of the Havilland Museum and focus cameras and microphones on Martin DePalma. With his flowing black mane, he's distinguished in an expensively tailored grey suit, silk cravat and diamond stickpin. He's used to primping and posing. Even without the crowd's additional cologne, scented hair spray and deodorant, DePalma alone would constitute perfumed sensory-overload.

"As the press release has indicated, the impregnable nature of our detection system and the immediate capture of this would-be thief by our alert security staff has precluded a successful attempt. You can see for yourself, the collection is still intact. The display will reopen with a minimum of delay."

"May we ask the value of the theft?"

"<u>Attempted</u> theft. Although the collection amounts to a great mass in volume, many are considered priceless. But the coins targeted are insured for seventeen million."

"But your publicity handout valued the entire collection at twenty-five million for the three thousand coins."

"That's correct."

"And the coins recovered totaled less than twenty, yet represent two thirds the entire value?"

"Well, the best and rarest are always more highly prized."

"What's the insurance company say about this?"

"Actually, as a result of such rapid apprehension, our rates, if anything, should be lowered."

"Mr. DePalma, have you determined how the thief gained access?"

"Yes, but for security reasons we will never disclose such information."

"Have you…?"

A young woman approaches and hands DePalma a note.

"I'm sorry, but you must excuse me. The collection is to be returned soon to Washington D.C., and I must make transport arrangements."

* * * * * *

The housekeeper, Lucinda's, spatulate, dimpled fingers tap a number code into the lock. She enters, cleans all horizontal surfaces and then washes clothes. On the back porch, ignoring the gamy odor, she mops and refills the pet food and water dishes.

* * * * * *

Behind a frosted glass door labeled "Detective Squad," Ryan—Irish good looks and bad temper—slams his fist onto the table, bouncing coffee cups. Sergeant Moore—footballer's heavy shoulders and narrow hips—smiles down at handcuffed Jimmy Doyle.

Doyle points a backward thumb toward Ryan. "What the hell's he mad at? I'm the one bein' booked."

"He just don' like you pullin' our chain."

"But I confessed."

"Confessed, hell. We caught you dead bang."

"Then what you hasslin' me for? Lock me up and let me get some sleep."

"Now you know we ain't gonna do that. Detective Ryan done explained it all to ya. We know you're not smart enough to pull this by yore lonesome."

"And I admitted I had a companion waiting for me outside."

Ryan picks up the conversation as if he's heard similar stories many times.

"There were no signs of forced entry. We know you had help getting in."

"Like I said. I hid in a packing crate 'til after closing."

"How'd you expect to sell the coins?"

"I been over this with you a dozen times. My partner had that covered."

"Yeah, some Fifth Avenue fence. But you don't know his name and never got his exact address. Only your partner knows that?"

"It was safer that way."

"And the name of your partner?"

"I never met him before and he wore a mask."

"Sure, and you wouldn't recognize him in a lineup? Couldn't tell him from your mama?"

"What is it with you guys? You all smell like glazed donuts, but you never share."

The two interrogators pull up short and regroup. "We'll take it again from the beginning."

CHAPTER-9
WHAT'S IN YOUR WALLET?

On the foredeck, aboard "Night Song," Kirk calls and adds a message to his answering machine. "I'm unavailable, but you can leave a message at the club. Back in time for Andrea." He makes another call, but a sudden gust of wind whips away his words.

Below deck, Melanie tears open a galley cabinet, finds and devours caviar, salsa, chips, chutney, marinated mushrooms, and brandied cherries. Like a Tasmanian Devil, she eats anything and everything, and at a hundred pounds, she never seems to gain an ounce. The only thing surviving her search-and-destroy mission is a box of disposable diapers. She looks sideways at him, all the while scanning the cabin for anything valuable to steal. "So, tell me about your ex."

While putting away the fresh linens, he answers, "We divorced three years ago. She lives across the river in Windsor."

"You're on good terms. Are you still in love with her?"

"No. I still love her. I always will. But I'm not in love with her."

"So what happened? She catch you with some stewardi aboard your little floating love nest here?"

"Not exactly."

"How not exactly?"

"Our team had just won the Diamond Jubilee Polo Open in Lexington. She was a nurse intern and couldn't join me. I'd had too much champagne, so after the

45

celebration, I turned in. But the team thought it would be fun to send up an expensive call girl."

She finds another cabinet and devours mandarin orange segments and stale oyster crackers. "Your wife...what's her name?"

"Jennifer."

"Jennifer managed to come down after all and caught you together?"

"Close enough. She found the girl in my room. I was passed out in bed. I can't say nothing happened. I have no recollection"

"She didn't believe you?"

"She took one look and walked out. I didn't find out the rest until I got home."

"The rest?"

"On the way out, she ran into the Argentine captain of the team we'd just beaten. He was a charmer and she took him to bed."

"To get back at you."

"Yeah. We didn't divorce when she told me. Only after she learned she was pregnant. I'd had a vasectomy so we knew who the father was. I told her I could handle it."

"But she couldn't. And Andrea is the child?"

"Right. Jennifer has a twice-a-month commitment to care for this rich old lady. I get along great with Andrea, so it works out for all concerned."

"You baby sit for free and take your ex-mother-in-law to lunch?"

"Well, when alimony was first set, I was making much less than I am now. I've renegotiated it up three times. Jennifer didn't want the extra money, so we agreed on a college fund for Andrea."

Shaking her head, Melanie mumbles to herself.

If only half of that is true, you are too good to be on the loose.

Moments later, Ethan climbs the gangway and knocks. Kirk pokes his head up through the transom without a word and takes the offered manila envelope. Ethan turns, steps off the deck, unties the boat and leaves. Kirk plays a CD and Fats Waller sings:

"KEEPIN' OUT OF MISCHIEF NOW."

A silent-running electric motor glides the boat to mid-harbor where Kirk drops anchor.

While he's busy up on deck, Melanie looks through his wallet. She finds credit cards, club membership cards and bankcards. She returns the cards, but puts three tens into her purse, then pours herself coffee. Unaware of the boat's motion, she mumbles to herself, *Huh, thirty dollars. Some tycoon.*

With her boots and purse in one hand, coffee in the other and a bunch of bananas under her arm, she steps up onto the deck.

Silhouetted against a dazzling sun, Kirk smiles at her.

She blinks, and backs to the rail. "Don't try to stop me."

"You have to do what you think is right."

"That's...right."

"Thirty bucks won't take you far."

"Far enough."

She lays her purse and boots on the deck, feels behind her for the lift section of rail leading to the gangway. She finds it and lifts.

"I'll get the money back to you."

"No big thing."

"Don't interfere or follow me."

"Wouldn't think of it." He watches her step back and plunge seven feet into the water. Spitting, sputtering and gasping, she surfaces and scrambles for the anchor chain. Bananas float all around her.

"Would you help me? I can't swim."

"You told me not to interfere."

"Please?"

"You were about to tell me about Mr. #207."

"I will, just—"

"Hold on a sec." Ducking below, he returns with bagel and coffee and pulls a deck chair to the rail. "Now we're both comfy. I turned off the phone so we wouldn't be interrupted."

A triangular dorsal fin appears and circles the flailing landlubber.

"K...I...R...K!"

"Don't scream, you'll scare the fish. About Mr. #207?"

"I was given a hundred-fifty-thousand down payment. The seven-hundred-thousand balance was to be paid when I delivered the coins to #207."

"What'd you do with the hundred-fifty thousand? You said you have no money, family or friends."

"I have...a lot of expenses."

"Besides food, I guess black ski masks and bullets cost a lot. What'd you do with the coins you stole?"

"I...hid them."

"Who was the guy in #207?"

"Don't know. I've never worked with anyone before. Never will again."

"Where'd you learn your trade? Cat Burglary 101 at CCNY?"

"I just...learned it. Now pull me up, damn it."

"What do you know about Jimmy Doyle, the guy they arrested after you'd switched the coins?"

"Nothing. I was told to wait near the 57th Street exit for a distraction that would set off the alarm, so I could slip out, and the open door wouldn't register."

"If you took the real coins, we can return them for a reward."

"Would they pay me more than eight-hundred-fifty thousand as reward?"

"I doubt it."

"Then I'm better off with my original deal."

"Whoever set this up never intended paying you the balance. If you hadn't been with me you too would be in a body bag."

"I might cut you in for a piece. Help me up and we'll talk a deal."

"Partners don't steal from each other."

The dorsal fins circle closer.

"Kirk, oh my God!"

"You don't have to call me God. Darling is enough, but you do have to stop this running-out nonsense."

"Anything, just..."

The triangular fins move closer.

"Have you ever done this before?"

"No!"

A seagull drops onto the deck, caws, steals his bagel and flies off.

"I can interpret animal language. He says you're lying."

The first dolphin nudges Melanie's arm, while the second dolphin swallows a banana. She SCREAMS.

Ignoring her panic, he says, "Another thing. You have to give up your life of crime."

"Bring me on board and we'll negotiate that part."

He drops the rope ladder over the side and jumps in. With her arms around his neck, he guides her to the ladder. "You look just like the first time we met."

"Hurry up, you fool."

"I'll have to teach you to swim, if you insist on these water sports."

CHAPTER-10
BURGLARY, THEFT AND BUNCO AS A HOBBY

Entering NYPD'S Burglary/Theft/Bunco division, Detective Ryan throws his file on top of a disorganized desk as Sergeant Moore hangs up the phone. "We know it was an inside job."
"But if no crime was committed, the D.A. won't back us up."
"A crime WAS committed, but because it was bungled so badly, we only have him on attempt."
"Might not even have that. If he never took the goods off the premises, his lawyer can say he was just admiring them in private."
"He was <u>stealing</u> them."
"I know that and you know that. But when we caught a guy in the supermarket aisle with a twelve-pound steak in his shorts and blood drippin' down his leg, what'd he always claim?"
"He was going to…"
"…pay at the counter."
"Right. If we only had more time."
"But we don't. Captain says close the case."

Over chopped chicken livers and red horseradish on a bagel from Boulangere Fantastique, Lieutenant Pisanti scans the text screen of his phone and shakes his head. "A union negotiator with no known criminal ties? That's a contradiction in terms."
The gray-haired detective sitting across from him asks, "What'd you say, Lou?"

"This Parkhurst gunshot victim from a Chicago suburb? His family says he had no plans to be in New York. He's supposed to be in San Diego at a submarine vet's reunion. It makes no sense."

He looks over the latest batch of crime scene photos. He sees something and calls the crime lab directly. "Martin, Lieutenant Pisanti here. I need you to punch up a print for me. I'll be up there in ten minutes."

"You kidding me? We're up to our ass in work. Try a week from Thursday."

"In that case, I'll be up there in five minutes."

Four minutes later, he climbs the stairs three at a time and bursts into the photo lab. He grabs a white smocked man, almost knocks the man's horn rim glasses off, drags him to a table and shoves a photo under a magnifier. "There's something under the body. Can you bring it up?"

"It's pretty light. Looks like fingernail scratches in the teak floor."

"That's what I thought, but I didn't see it at the scene. It was under a pool of blood."

"I'll do what I can. Maybe under ultra-violet."

"Get me another frontal of the victim too. I need to check with the Lake Pleasant Department."

"Have it sometime this afternoon. You still owe me from that last blood work-up."

"I'll bring you an autographed photo of Lady GaGa."

"Oh PLEASE! I deal with enough weird and bizarre things as it is. Make it Sofia Vergara and you got a deal."

* * * * * *

Dressed only in a man's shirt, Melanie chooses from the assortment of Levi cutoffs and small size deck shoes offered in the main stateroom closet. The guest bathroom offers at least twelve different women's perfumes. She bends wire coat hangers into forms to dry her bra and panties.

Up on deck. Kirk studies a folder. The first item is a museum blowup of a coin captioned, "Brasher Doubloon—the most valuable coin in the collection on exhibit this week-end."

He dials Ethan, "I want everything the police have on the man murdered in #207. My address." He punches off. Melanie brings sliced pineapple, green chips, salsa and margaritas, and then sits across from him, and puts her bare feet into his lap.

He asks, "How much do you know about the goods you purloined?"

"I know they were going to pay me a lot of money to snatch them."

"Not really so much, considering their real value. The coins you took were all unique or so rare that only a handful exist."

"But how could they expect such rare items to find a market? Potential buyers would know they were stolen. They could never be displayed, insured or sold."

"If the intent was ransom, only the original owner would be told about the switch."

"But that's all changed with Doyle's arrest. So where does he fit into the plan?"

She wriggles her toes. "I don't know, unless he was an independent, hired as back up in case I failed."

"So he stole the phonies you planted."

"But they were recovered in time."

"Sooner or later an expert will realize they're fakes."

"What is it, a franchise? Like Dairy Queen or White Castle? Purloined Coins-R-Us? That kind of thing?"

While filling her mouth with food, she gives him a dirty look and at the same time, rubs her bare feet against his groin.

He rolls his eyes and says, "You must have the metabolism of a ferret."

* * * * * *

The phone rings at the Barelli, Foster and Quan Law Offices. Dan Barelli—dark and swarthy, holds an open folder; Jimmy Doyle's photo is attached to the arrest record. He speaks into the phone, "That's right Mr..." PAUSE. "But this is a secure line and we're using the scrambler, so..." PAUSE. "I understand. Anyway, sir, I've taken care of that little matter. He's been arraigned. The trial date will be set as soon as..." PAUSE. "I'm not sure that I can..." PAUSE. "One million last year." PAUSE. "No sir, my partners wouldn't like to lose that kind of retainer." PAUSE. "That...won't be necessary. I'll see to it."

CHAPTER-11
STYXX AND STONES

In the main stateroom of the seventy-five foot yacht, "STYXX," with the portholes locked and covered by heavy drapes, the interior is warm, but smells deeply of damp salt air. Smoking Jacket smiles, hangs up the phone and inspects a tray of coins. The first coin is a Brasher Doubloon.

* * * * * *

Captain Younger dials. "Lieutenant Pisanti? Captain Younger, Lake Pleasant P.D. I just got your package." PAUSE. "Yes, quite a problem, in fact. The body you have is not the man in your document." PAUSE. "No, not even close." PAUSE. "I just had donuts and coffee with Charles Blakely. He's been at an American Legion reunion In San Diego." PAUSE. "He's a family man, affluent, well known and liked."

Ethan is shown to Lieutenant Pisanti's desk. "Ethan Brown, Data Intercept, I'm working with Atlantic Mutual; checking that Parkhurst male cauc, Blakely, Charles. We'd like to verify cause of death. Suicide makes a huge difference with the insurance."

Lieutenant Pisanti looks down at the coroner's report and photo of the man listed as Charles Blakely.

"We've no question on that, but there IS good reason to hold up payment."

"Oh?"

"It seems our D.B. is <u>not</u> your insured." As he studies the folder, Ethan reads it upside down.

"Leave your number and I'll keep you updated. There may be a fraud case to be filed on."

"Thank you, Lieutenant." In the hallway, from memory, Ethan, in red ink, hastily copies the remembered data into a notebook.

Antonio Maretti, two convictions, receiving stolen goods. Buffalo, N.Y. 1986 and 1991. Paroled from Dannemorra, Jan, this year.

Sergeant Moore and Detective Ryan watch in impotent fury as Jimmy Doyle is released from custody and escorted down the stairs by a very expensively dressed man.

Ethan enters, shows a press pass to Sergeant Moore.

"Anything new on Jimmy Doyle?"

"Yesterday's news."

"You mean because he confessed?"

"I mean because Barelli, Forster and Quan just bailed him out."

"That means Big money. They don't handle penny-ante hustlers like Doyle."

"Twenty million is penny-ante?"

"He's spent a total of fifteen years in Dannemorra. All for piss-ant stuff. P.D. defended him each time. What do you make of that?"

"We don' make nothin' of it. D.A.'s handlin' the case. We're out of it."

"So you think there's somebody behind this, keeping in the shadows?"

"And we'll probly, never bring him into daylight."

"Look, if you want me to keep this low profile..."

"No, in fact, you might just shake the right bush."

"Sounds like a plan."

56

* * * * * *

Kirk and Melanie enter the Havilland Museum closet just as DePalma leaves his office. Melanie hoists herself up on Kirk's shoulders, lifts the ceiling panel and reaches in, but finds nothing.

"You're sure that's where you left them?"

She gives him a dirty look. You think I'm careless with merchandise worth twenty million dollars?"

"Okay, okay, just asking."

"Well don't be stupid. Boost me higher."

He holds her by the ankles and presses her higher. "What do you see?"

"No damn coins, but…wait, let me down."

"Is this another of your little games?"

"If I had them, we wouldn't still be here. Every exposure is a possible trap. We need some scotch tape."

He lets her down. "Why?"

"Because there are fingerprints up there in the dust."

"Probably yours."

"I wore gloves. This is not my first rodeo. Besides, I never reached that far in."

"Then they must belong to whoever got the coins after you left them."

"By Jove, Sherlock, I think you've solved the case." She opens the door and looks out. He follows her into the corridor. She listens at DePalma's door. Before Kirk realizes what she's doing, she's picked the lock and pulled him inside after her.

"Hey, I don't think…"

"Sssh…let me do the thinking. You just look macho and keep your eye on the door."

She quickly searches, finds no coins and no scotch tape.

57

CHAPTER-12
WILDLIFE IN THE BIG CITY

Kirk leads Melanie into Midnight Blue, a dimly lit bar across the greensward from the yacht harbor. He orders two bowls of clam chowder and signs a tab. "If they didn't tear up #207, they already had the coins, or knew they weren't to be found there. So they went to the Parkhurst <u>only</u> to kill both of you and eliminate any connection."

"AND…cheat me out of my money! Jacob Golden, a Buffalo attorney was the intermediary. I'll kill that slime bag."

"How do you know him?"

"I…just know him."

He dials the bar phone. "Ethan, I want low profile in-depth on a Buffalo attorney, Jacob Golden." Hanging up, he slides the phone to Melanie. She seems reluctant to call, but he stares her down. She calls, but holds the receiver away from him.

"Mr. Golden, Melanie. I want to know with whom you set me up and what the hell happened."

"Miss Winterhalter, I'm sorry things took an unpleasant turn, but then the best of plans sometimes go awry and, as I explained, I would not reveal the other principal's identity to you any more than I would yours to him."

"But…"

"By the way, I received your last hundred and fifty thousand. Now the balance…?"

"I'll get back to you on that." She hangs up and gives Kirk an innocent stare and an unconvincing smile. "Said he didn't know anything."

He feeds the jukebox and stares at her while Fats Waller sings:

"IT'S A SIN TO TELL A LIE."

With a determined step, she heads toward the "Night Song."

"What are you going to do?"

"Find those coins."

"How?"

"Somebody at that museum knows where they are and I'm going to nail his hide to the wall."

"You'll just march in and say, 'Hi, I was hired to rip off your coins but things were messed up. One man went to jail and another man was killed. So if whoever took my coins will just give them back to me I'll be very grateful.'"

"Something like that, maybe not quite as politely. I've still got my gun, you know."

"No you don't. You left it at my apartment."

"You'll get it for me. These people have my money and tried to kill me. I'll bet if that happened to you, it would even perturb Mr. Nice Guy."

"Sure, but I wouldn't go off half-cocked."

"I'll think of something.

"Waving a gun at the museum like Clint Eastwood?"

"Look, if you think I'm so stupid you'd probably be better off without me cluttering up your life."

"No question about it."

"So, I'll just be toddling off."

"Can't toddle now."

"Why not?"

"We haven't solved the case yet."

"WE? There's no we. I'll get my money and be on my way."

"Where? To Buffalo?"

"N...o. What makes you say that?"

"Just a guess. Well, go ahead if you're going." PAUSE. "Of course I'll have to tell the police everything."

"Who are you, Mr. New York City Public Spirit?"

"No. I just want to keep us both out of jail."

"Okay, but you don't have to mention me."

"Not much of a story without you."

"They wouldn't know who I am. You don't even know that."

"They'll find your prints all over my apartment."

"What do you want, a cut of the money? I never promised that. We were just talking."

"Plus, you have a very attractive big toe."

"Say what?"

"I don't want to see it decorated by a toe tag."

"So how will I get my money?"

"I haven't worked that out. But then, I don't have all the data yet."

"Data? I don't want data. I want to kick some ass."

"That's fine when you know whose ass to kick."

"You're all talk."

He pulls her roughly to him and kisses her.

"Well, I didn't mean that part." She follows him across the grass toward the "Night Song." Along the way, he stops to pick up a small brown and white lump and holds a shivering young owl.

"What are you going to do with that? We can't eat it. It's an owl, for crying out loud."

"It'd be all right if it was an ostrich? A peacock?"

"A peahen maybe, yes."

CHAPTER-13
NATURAL-LY

Lieutenant Pisanti pushes the button at #702. Fats Waller and Lucinda respond.

"Mr...?"

"Boss ain't here."

"Lieutenant Pisanti, NYPD Homicide. May I ask you a question?

"You just did."

"Yes, well, when may I speak with your employer?"

"When he's here. That's two questions. You got a bunch more? I don't get paid for jawin' with cops."

"No. I thank you for your help. You might say that I was here and..."

She walks away in mid-sentence, leaving him to talk to a three inch, steel-clad door.

Next at #207, he unlocks the crime scene padlock and enters. At the chalk-marked outline of the body, he moves his flashlight into various positions, while he goes over the hardwood floor with a magnifying glass. Finally in one light setting he finds faint fingernail scratches and brings up "Mark V..." On his list of tenants he finds a Marcus Voskopf, #603.

He knocks at #603, receives no answer. Marc Voskopf is apparently out.

* * * * * *

Melanie looks up at the PARKSIDE VETERINARY HOSPITAL sign, turns angrily to Kirk. "What are we doing here? I already have a driver's license and you've no need for one."

"D.V.M. means Doctor of Veterinary Medicine, not the Department of Motor vehicles."

"Oh, right."

A white-smocked young man holds up an X-ray, taps it with a fingertip and speaks over his shoulder. "The wing is a clean break. We can set it, but..."

Melanie shakes her head. "I told him it was crazy."

"Well, not many people bring me predators. There are special problems."

Kirk hands the nurse a platinum bankcard. She runs it through the machine. Melanie takes scotch tape and a glass slide from the table.

"Wild animals don't always respond to captive care."

Kirk takes back his card. "Call when he's ready to be picked up."

* * * * * *

At Havilland, Ethan is shown into DePalma's office. "Ryan Montgomery, Smithsonian Publicity. I have a few questions about the robbery. We should speak in private, to keep it all low profile."

"There's nothing to discuss. I've given the particulars to—"

"You've not seen the papers?"

"No, what...?"

Ethan hands him the folded newspaper under his arm. He reads the headline,

"Questions Arise Surrounding Abortive Museum Robbery."

"Naturally, Mr. DePalma, we want to down-play this as much as possible."

He frowns. "Would you excuse me a moment?"

"Of course."

He leaves, and Ethan takes the opportunity to do a hasty search of the desk drawers.

DePalma returns and stares at Ethan. "Who are you? The Smithsonian knows nothing about you."

"Oh, you must have called the main switchboard. I'm at the Silver Hill complex. I'll have the section head verify my credentials as soon as I get back to the office."

"We'll just wait, then, for authorization."

"As you wish. I had hoped to stave off unwanted publicity, but…" He leaves and makes quick red ink notes in his notebook. Pulling his car out of the parking lot, he's followed by Long Cigar and Hearing Aid.

* * * * * *

Inside the closet, Kirk again presses Melanie high above his head. She uses Scotch tape to transfer the fingerprints to her glass slide. Kirk whispers, "I have a microscope aboard."

Again she leads Kirk into DePalma's immaculate office. From the desk, she carefully slips a single glass with red wine stains into a paper bag. Inside a credenza, stuffed behind newspapers, Kirk finds a laptop computer with a thumb drive and TV camera; its mounting bracket and screws still hold plaster chips. He slips the thumb drive into his pocket.

CHAPTER-14
STYXX AHOY

Smoking Jacket answers a call. "No, I have another bidder, up to five million. He wants that coin. After all, it is the only breast-chop Doubloon. If you don't want it…" PAUSE. "Fine. I know you'll enjoy it." He hangs up and, wearing latex gloves, replaces the Brasher Doubloon in a velvet tray, takes it to a wall safe, and places it atop a similar tray with a dozen identical breast-chop Brasher Doubloons.

* * * * * *

Aboard "Night Song," Melanie lifts her eyes from the microscope and frowns. "Damn! DePalma's prints don't match those from the closet."

"Well, it was a logical guess."

"Gets us no closer to those coins."

"Oh! I forgot. I found this in DePalma's office." He takes the thumb drive from his jacket pocket.

"What is it?"

"Don't know and I don't have a computer or TV aboard."

"I know. You have other forms of entertainment. I found your bimbo wardrobe."

"That's—"

"Don't rationalize. C'mon, let's get a look at that thing."

* * * * * *

Blocks from police headquarters, homeless street people lead police to a debris box; they find a dead Jimmy Doyle, a single .45 caliber hole in his chest. He smells bad, but at least the hole has stopped bleeding.

* * * * * *

Lieutenant Pisanti rings the Parkhurst doorbell at #603. Marcus, opens the door and smiles into the hallway.

"Mr. Voskopf? Lieutenant Pisanti, Homicide. May I have a little of your time?"

"Of course, please come in. I was just about to have dinner. Would you care to join me? It is simple fare, Hungarian goulash. A young woman in brass just shared it with me."

"Thank you, no. Brass?"

He admits Lieutenant Pisanti into an antique-filled apartment. Photos of orchestras and shelved busts of classical composers fill one wall. Grand piano and bass violin stand ready and Mozart's

"A LITTLE NIGHT MUSIC"

plays from large corner speakers. "I'm sorry; we live in our own isolated world and assume everyone knows what we mean."

"You're...a musician?"

"New York Philharmonic. May I offer you some wine?" He pours Hungarian Green into two glasses.

"Thank you. I'm unfamiliar with wine or classical music. Sorry."

"Don't be. It's like classical literature. Many admit they'd love to have read it, but don't ever actually read it."

"Can you tell me where you were last Sunday from nine P.M. to midnight?"

"I hope so. I was playing the non-waltzing Strauss at the U.N. Rotunda. It was a televised UNICEF fundraiser. I was on stage from seven until we closed with Don Quixote." He feels for a program from the table and holds it out upside down.

The Atlantic Pops presents an evening of Richard Strauss with Marcus Voskopf, renowned cello soloist.

"Excuse me; I didn't realize it before. You're…"

"Blind is the word you're tactfully seeking. Yes, but it doesn't affect music and that's my entire life."

"Well, I thank you for your time, Mr. Voskopf." He rises and heads for the door.

"Perhaps, Lieutenant, you and a friend would be my guest at the symphony. This week we're doing Mozart."

"Yes, I'd appreciate that." He takes the offered tickets, then hesitates. "Do you know any of the other tenants, Mr. Voskopf?"

"All of them. Some very well. How may I be of help?"

"You might ask the tenant in #702 to speak with me."

"You want to speak with Kirk? Yes, of course."

Moments later, Lucinda answers to Fats Waller and sees Voskopf and the Lieutenant on the closed circuit TV.

"Lieutenant Pisanti needs to speak to Kirk, Lucinda."

69

"I know you all right, Mr. Voskoppi, but I don't let nobody in when Mr. Cannard not here."

The Lieutenant leans toward the door. "Would you have Mr. Cannard contact me as soon as possible, please?"

"Soon's I see him."

Voskopf shrugs at the lieutenant. They meet Ethan at the elevator.

"C'mon, kid; you can ride with me. I'll tell you what I can."

CHAPTER-15
PARKHURST FROM THE OUTSIDE

Long Cigar and Hearing Aid watch from the black Continental as Lieutenant Pisanti and Ethan enter the police car together. Long Cigar holds a tenant list; all are checked off except for Voskopf and Kirk. Long Cigar checks his .45, pins a phony police badge to his lapel. "Let's go see." Hearing Aid folds his newspaper. "I think we oughtta go check."

They reach the front door just as a woman, burdened with Saks bags fumbles with her key. They carry her bags and escort her to her apartment on ten.

"Thank you, officers. I've always said New York has the very finest."

"Our pleasure, ma'am."

They're barely gone when she sprays room freshener, trying to kill the obnoxious cigar smell.

* * * * * *

Kirk and Melanie get off the elevator on seven as Long Cigar and Hearing Aid, on ten, take the same elevator down to six.

They ring Voskopf's bell. No answer. Long Cigar frowns. "Let's go 'round to the service entrance."

Hearing Aid says, "Let's try the back way."

"Yeah, good idea."

From the service hall, they break into Voskopf's empty apartment. They search, but find no sign of Melanie. Disturbing furniture in the process, they leave a trail of blue smoke.

* * * * * *

Kirk works his apartment's coded lock. He and Melanie enter. Lucinda is busy removing prescription pills from a dozen bottles. "Police has been here. Homicide Lieutenant Pissenanti wants to talk to ya."
"Did he say what he wanted?"
Melanie pulls his sleeve. "Let's get the hell out while the getting's—"
"Said he wants to talk to ya. I'm going to get an MRI while I have the strength to fight off whatever fatal disease I have."
Kirk packs extra clothes. Melanie reads the titles on his nightstand, all self-help books. She folds her dress, then brings two snifters of brandy, gives Kirk one. They drink, obviously toasting something. She finds her .25 in the drawer, slips it into her purse; Kirk takes it away, locks it in a large wall safe. Melanie searches the freezer. She takes out frozen waffles and munches one while reading a telegram from the wastebasket.

Kirk Cannard, Parkhurst #702, Manhattan, N.Y.
Kirk, tonight would be a mistake STOP
You don't want a serious relationship STOP
Go to the ball without me STOP
You might meet someone there who can live without a long-term commitment STOP
Karen

Fats Waller sings:

"AIN'T MISBEHAVIN'"

On the closed circuit, Melanie sees a dazzling smile on a beautiful blonde in American Airlines uniform. With the stolen door code, she opens the door only a crack.

"Hi, is Kirk in? I'm Karen."

"Oh, you must be his much older sister. The office sent word to the family. We've sprayed the apartment so—"

"W…ho are you?"

"Nurse Kravitz, Department of Health, Communicable Disease Division. I think it's safe now, if you wanna come in. I've got extra gloves and masks."

"I think…Not!"

"Should I tell Kirk that you called?"

"Don't bother."

Melanie shuts the door, turns and answers Kirk's raised eyebrows with "Jehovah's Witness. I said you'd surveyed, found you'd be number 400,001 and figured the lottery was a better bet."

He smiles, locks the door behind them and leads her to the elevator. She still carries the brandy decanter under her arm.

CHAPTER-16
BACK AT…WELL, IF YOU'VE BEEN PAYING ATTENTION, YOU KNOW

Long Cigar and Hearing Aid hesitate. Kirk's door poses an obviously challenge. Hearing Aid reads Long Cigar's lips. "I'll go 'round back. You ring the bell. I'll listen. If nobody answers, I'll go in."

He nods and waits at the front door. Long Cigar breaks into the communal service area.

Hearing Aid pushes the button. Hearing no sound, he waits.

Long Cigar hears Fats Waller, but no answering sounds. He tries the door, but fails to get it open. Then he sees the pet door. Lit by night-light only, Long Cigar, on hands and knees, reaches a hand through and bumps a food dish, scattering kibble. A squat black and grey body clamps a mouthful of teeth around the hand. Long Cigar flops like a hooked trout. Unnoticed, his .45 falls. Screaming in pain, he twists, pulls, fights, but can't retract his hand.

At the front door, unaware of trouble, Hearing Aid, picking his teeth and burping, watches.

Long Cigar finally carries a bleeding hand to rejoin Hearing Aid. Deep puncture marks form a parabolic shape. Hearing Aid plugs his earpiece in place. "Why the hell didn't you yell?"

With his good hand, Long Cigar bitch-slaps his partner on the back of the head and through clenched teeth, says, "Get me to a doctor quick, before I bleed to death."

"I don't think you can bleed to death just from a thing like that. Rabies, yeah. Boy, I never seen a rat bite this big. Besides, we can't go to no saw bones. He'd ask where you got the injury."

"Then find me a vet. I might need a distemper or tetanus shot."

"Probly both. Then there's bubonic plague. That's a definite possibility. But I don't think they got a shot for that. I think ya just better plan ta die."

With mail under his arm, Marcus Voskopf enters #603 and instantly notes the misplaced furniture and cigar smoke. He dials 911. "Lieutenant Pisanti, Homicide, please. He left just a few moments ago. This is Marcus Voskopf. Someone has just broken into my apartment."

* * * * * *

The Lieutenant listens to the relay on his car phone. He makes a mid-block U-turn and nods at Ethan to toggle the red lights and siren switches.

Hearing Aid pulls the Continental from the curb. Not hearing the siren, he almost runs into Pisanti's police car.

* * * * * *

In Central Park, Kirk's beeper goes off. "That's the vet's number. I told him to call." He flags down a Hansom Cab.

* * * * * *

Long Cigar and Hearing Aid leave the Parkside Veterinary Hospital and are climbing into the Continental. Long Cigar's hand is bandaged like a wrapped ham. The car door partially closes on it. Just as he's about to scream in pain, the Hansom pulls up. Kirk and Melanie climb out and enter the vet's office.

"Hey, that's her, so that guy must be him."

"I can't do anything right now, my hand is throbbing like crazy. Besides, I can't find my gun. Let's wait and follow them."

"It's too crowded, let's get 'er later, when they leave."

"Good plan. I don't know why I didn't think of it."

* * * * * *

At "Night Song," Karen slips aboard. Hiding the burning tip of her cigarette from sight, she sits in the aft deck shadows and smokes.

* * * * * *

Inside the vet's office, Kirk holds the caged owl high above his head. The owl blinks, flexes long, razor sharp talons.

"He's really not ready to go. The painkillers will keep him sedated for another few hours. I'm sorry, but he's got all the other patients so nervous, we just can't keep him any longer."

Melanie has an-'I told you so look on her face'. "See, from the start, I said this was crazy."

The vet says, "Two drops of this liquid in his water every twelve hours will keep him sedated until he's ready to be released. You'll also need to catch him a mouse at least once a day. He likes them fresh."

Melanie grimaces, "You mean live? Yuk."

Kirk grins at her, "I'll get you a net. It'll keep you too busy to worry about anything else."

"Get real."

Waiting for a cab, Melanie looks obviously annoyed at his doing anything not related to <u>her</u> problem. A cab pulls up out front and HONKS.

CHAPTER-17
COUNTING COUP

In "Night Song's" galley, Melanie makes herself a sardine and strawberry sandwich as Kirk sees the young owl comfortably ensconced below deck. He spreads newspaper under the cage. She drinks brandy from the decanter and offers it to Kirk.

"No. More than one drink makes me aggressive." His beeper goes off again.

She pours his drink into a snifter glass and doubles it. "Damn, we never played your thumb drive."

"We've got to see Ethan anyway. He'll have a laptop."

* * * * * *

Ethan dials Kirk's number. "Ah, Mr. Nightsong. I'm here working with Lieutenant Pisanti, NYPD. Marcus Voskopf's apartment has been broken into. It may be connected to one of the cases I'm on. We should communicate. I'll be here at least a half hour." He hangs up and watches the Lieutenant dust for prints, as Marcus serves them Viennese coffee.

* * * * * *

Half a block away, Long Cigar sees the burning cigarette from the aft deck, but can't get a clear shot.

* * * * * *

On Parkhurst's tenth floor, Mrs. Burns opens her door to Kirk.

"I hate to trouble you, Mrs. Burns, but they're painting my place and my cousin is allergic to the fumes. Could she stay here while I go down and get a few things?"

"No trouble at all, Kirk, dear. But, cousin? Really? What kind of scam is this, you rascal?"

"I'm afraid I don't know what you mean."

"Oh, you scamp. You know the police were here looking for this young lady. Not that good looking hunk, but the other two, the ones that helped me with my packages not an hour ago. One with that horrid cigar and the other one with the distant look."

Moments later, at #603, Kirk is admitted by Ethan. He sees Marcus and the Lieutenant.

"Hi, I'm Kirk Cannard. You're Lieutenant Pisananiti?

"Lieutenant Pisanti. Please come in, Mr. Cannard."

"My housekeeper says you have some questions?"

"Yes, some of your neighbors tell me that around midnight last Sunday you were carrying a friend home. And that you might have come from #207. Is that about how you remember it?"

"That's close, but we were both a little under the weather or I wouldn't have been trying to carry her up six flights."

"Just a minute. Six? You're on seven."

"Right. That's six flights up."

"Oh, yes. Well, did you know the tenant in #207?"

"No, why? Did he steal the rugs and light bulbs?"

"I beg your pardon?"

"'Did I know,' infers he moved out. Why else are the police interested if he didn't steal something?"

"He didn't move out. Then you weren't coming from apartment #207?"

"Why would I be coming from the apartment of a person I don't know? What's happened here, Marcus?"

"Burglary, I guess. Inept thieves, it seems. They got nothing"

"Lucky. I suppose the door was locked."

"Maybe something other than luck. Have you been to your own apartment yet, Mr. Cannard?"

"No, why, Lieutenant?"

"I'd like to know if this was the only unit broken into."

"You're welcome to come up with me and look for yourself."

"Thank you."

Kirk opens his high security door and stands aside to allow Lieutenant Pisanti and Ethan to enter.

"Oh," Lieutenant Pisanti holds up a single black suede shoe. "Does this by any chance belong to your friend?"

"I don't know. Where'd you find it?"

"In the hallway."

"I'll ask her, if you like."

Kirk turns on the stereo. Fats Waller sings:

"YOUR FEETS TOO BIG."

"Uh, Lieutenant, are you the only investigator on this case, whatever it is?"

"Yes. Why do you ask?"

"Just curious." *So you'd know if any other investigators were working the same ground.*

"Lieutenant, may I offer you a pair of polo match tickets without it looking like a bribe?"

"Do you have any reason to bribe me?"

"Of course not."

"Great. I've never seen a polo match."

The Lieutenant looks through Kirk's unit. Ethan points out the spilled water, scattered food, scratches on the access door and blood drops on the floor. They find the .45.

"Is this your gun, Mr. Cannard?"

"Nope. It seems to have been left by someone in a hurry. Look at the blood trail."

The lieutenant leaves and Kirk leads a disgruntled Melanie from Mrs. Burns' door.

"Hum! It took you long enough. What'd you do, turn me in for the reward?"

"What reward? I'm the only one crazy enough to even want you, much less pay money for you."

She seems slightly mollified. "Let's go back to that bar of yours. They had good clam chowder. I might even start to eat normally."

"Well, today they have—"

"What? Now, you don't want to take me? Okay, I'm sorry. I shouldn't have accused you."

"No, it's just—"

"I'll be on my best behavior. Honest." Her kiss is surely intended to show her honesty. On some it might have worked.

CHAPTER-18
NOW AREN'T YOU GLAD YOU READ THIS FAR?

Kirk and Melanie enter Midnight Blue in the midst of a lingerie show in progress. Several of the models wave at Kirk. One very attractive tall blonde in ultra-skimpy red bra and panties slides up to him. She pirouettes, shows a lot of cleavage and lays a hand familiarly on his arm.

"Haven't seen you in a long time, lover. You likee this outfit?"

Melanie frowns. "We would, honey. If it came in anything but the Big Mama sizes." She disdainfully casts the blonde's hand from Kirk's arm and pulls him outside. She hugs him and says, "I'll fix you something special at home."

He doesn't put up much of a fight.

They stroll the water's edge toward the Fair Winds Yacht Club. At an abandoned rope locker, he pulls her inside.

"We need to get dinner for the raptor."

"W…hat."

At a pile of rotting planks, he stops. "There should be some tender morsels here. Look underneath."

"Look, you're not being funny. That's just a warped sense of humor."

A few yards away, Long Cigar and Hearing Aid creep along outside the yacht club's cyclone fence. They see a glowing cigarette and movement aboard "Night

Song" and mistake Karen for Melanie. With his bandaged hand, Long Cigar reaches for his gun, but it's missing.

"I lost my gun. Gimme yours."

"Whattdaya mean, lost yours?"

"Don't argue. Just gimme a piece."

"You the one wanted me to carry." He hands Long Cigar a small nickel-plated pistol."

"What the hell's this? A .32? Damn ladies gun."

"Yeah, fine weapon. Belonged to my ma. It maybe wasn't blessed by the priest like your .45, but it's kosher."

Long Cigar takes aim, flinches as he fires. A bullet whizzes past Karen's ear and she falls back over the rail into the water.

"Got her. Let's get the hell away from here. Water makes me nervous."

Hearing Aid frowns and says, "Maybe that's cause you got rabies after all. It's called hydra-fobious'"

At the SHOT, Kirk and Melanie move to a dirty window. They see a dark figure swimming off at Olympic speed.

Long Cigar and Hearing Aid run past the warehouse and drive off in the Continental

Kirk turns and asks, "Did you see the license plate?"

"Yeah. XXYTS, but that's stupid. It doesn't mean anything."

He gives her a questioning look, then realizes what she means.

* * * * * *

In his office, Lieutenant Pisanti reads the lab report, then excitedly dials the phone.

"Gimme Burglary/Theft/Bunco. Whoever's in charge of that Havilland Museum heist." PAUSE. "Yeah, Sergeant, Lieutenant Pisanti, Homicide. I've got the gun killed Jimmy Doyle. It's tied to another homicide I'm working on." PAUSE. "I haven't made the connection yet. I thought at first a woman was involved, but now I don't know. Call me in the morning. Let's put our heads together over coffee."

* * * * * *

In an unfamiliar neighborhood, Kirk and Melanie finally stop running from a possible encounter with Long Cigar and Hearing Aid. Kirk buys oranges from a street merchant. Melanie is dragging. She slumps in a heap on the steps of the Third Baptist Church. "I can't walk another foot. Don't bother about me. I'll just expire right here."

"With all your exercising, I figured you to be more durable."

"I'm not used to being shot at, starved, almost drowned, or forced on fifty-mile marches."

"You should be, in your line of work. And nobody's shot at you."

"They meant it for me. Twice!"

He looks up, sees the church lights are on. He pulls her up the steps.

"It's a good sign. We'll go in and get help."

"I'm Catholic."

"I thought you were a pragmatist, but whatever. Do you worship a different God than they do?"

"Well no, but…"

Inside, Kirk tries to remain inconspicuous as Melanie faces a sea of black faces in the midst of choir practice. Reverend Waters a huge black man approaches. "How may I be of service to you, my children?"

"Didn't mean to interrupt, Padre. We just wanted to pray and then slip out."

The pastor looks at Melanie's boat clothes and disheveled appearance.

"I sense you need physical as well as spiritual help."

To the choir's rendition of, "Were You There When They Crucified My Lord," Kirk adds a clear baritone voice and is acknowledged. Melanie and Reverend Waters listen with rapt attention. The choir disbands. Several members welcome them and offer to show them to an adjacent canteen area. Kirk accepts coffee and a donut. Melanie opts for the red beans, rice, corn bread and ribs."

Reverend Waters shows them to the basement and introduces the Homeless Shelter Director. "We still have room. Men sleep in the west wing, women in the east."

Melanie balks. "That's okay. We'll make other arrangements, but thanks." She drags Kirk outside. Right up the block, they see a boy removing personal items from an ancient VW van with Oregon plates. There's an abandoned vehicle sticker on the windshield.

Kirk says to the boy, "Suck a valve?"

"Yeah. Wouldn't be so bad, but HP made me drive it off the interstate. Been nursin' it since Ohio. Now I can't afford to move it, so I'm gonna' lose it."

Through dark curtains, Kirk sees a clean foam mattress. "What do you figure it's worth?"

"Nothin', but I just spent three-hundred dollars on new rubber."

"I'll give you a hundred for it, as-is. Hubcap shop up the street should give you two hundred for the wheels."

"Deal."

Kirk pays him and helps Melanie inside. The boy jacks up the car and removes the wheels.

* * * * * *

Long Cigar enters the donut shop, grabs a free glazed donut sample and heads for the back corner phones. He speaks softly. "Yeah, we got the woman. She was with a guy named Kirk Cannard." PAUSE. "Yeah, but…" PAUSE. "I don't see what difference it makes now. With her gone, he can't…" PAUSE. "Yeah, but…" PAUSE. "Yeah, but…" PAUSE. "Yes, sir." He hangs up and turns to Hearing Aid.

"What?"

Exasperated, Long Cigar drags him away from his second maple bar.

CHAPTER-19
WHO'S ON FIRST?

Aboard "Night Song," Long Cigar disconnects the power. They're in the pitch black interior.

Hearing Aid complains. "How we gonna prove we got her if we don't find the body?" From below comes, "WHOO."

"The girl, that's whoo."

"Well why are you tellin' me that? Like I didn't know."

"Then why did you ask?"

"I didn't..."

"Whoo."

"The girl, that's who."

"Sh...the guy must be below deck. He may have a gun. I'll go down, while you watch up here."

"Why don't I wait here while you go down and check?"

Long Cigar slips quietly down the dark ladder to the salon. He's even less graceful than in Voskopf's dry land apartment. Bumping and cursing, he stumbles around in the dark. A dropped frying pan sounds like a gunshot, then there's more bumping and expletives. He ascends the ladder, carrying the owl's cage onto the deck. It HOOTS. Hearing Aid opens the cage. "Oh, what a cute little birdy." He reaches inside and YEOWLS in pain.

From above, a brace of crows dive on the owl. In the confusion, Long Cigar is attacked and bitten. Both men cower and try to find shelter. There is none except the open water. They take the only escape offered them.

* * * * * *

Past midnight, two youths, using snips and wrenches, work quickly to cut the VW engine from its shroud. In the doing, they jostle the car.

Melanie shakes Kirk awake. "Did we drive to California?"

"No, why?"

"We're having an earthquake."

"Things that go bump in the night? Don't be ridiculous. You had a nightmare."

"No, there's another one."

"Probably someone stealing the engine."

"And you took my gun. Do something."

"Why? It's no good. Go back to sleep."

The van stops rocking and a SCRAPING sound slowly diminishes.

Melanie is too hyper to sleep and can't stand the idea that Kirk can. She shakes him. "What are you going to do about this mess you got me into?"

"Me?"

She takes a swig of brandy from the silver-topped decanter, offers him some. He takes a long drink and frowns at her.

"If you hadn't been home, I'd have discovered the error and gone down to #207."

"You'd have been murdered."

"Right, and I wouldn't be going through all this stress now." With three stiff fingers, she pokes him in the ribs. "It's all your fault."

"I'm working on a plan. I'll tell you in the morning."

"Tell me now. I can't sleep anyway."

Kirk finishes explaining his plan.

She finds the oranges, digs a hole in one and loudly sucks the juice. Kirk tries unsuccessfully to cover his ears.

Throwing the last of the juiceless oranges away, she smiles. "I like it. Even if it doesn't work it's better than doing nothing. Now I can sleep."

"Yeah, but now I'm wide-awake."

She puts the decanter to his lips, waits until he's taken his second drink, and then pulls him over on top of her. "Knock yourself out, cowboy."

CHAPTER-20
OH, IT HURTS SO BAD

A short time later at Parkside Veterinary Hospital, Hearing Aid shoves a throbbing finger the size and color of a garlic sausage under the nose of a sleepy eyed vet. "This here's a owl bite."
 The vet looks and yawns. "One of the nicest I've ever seen."
 He reaches for a four-ounce bottle and a hypodermic needle about the size they use to give massive shots to horses.
 "Whadda ya gonna do with that?"
 "Rabies is a definite worry with wild animal bites."
 Hearing Aid starts to stand, but, ungracefully, faints into a heap. Long Cigar laughs. He wrestles with his own news and finally says, "Yeah, an' we was attacked by some kinda vultures." He exhibits numerous slash cuts. The vet reaches for another bottle of liquid. Long Cigar faints.

* * * * * *

A city tow truck hooks the VW's front bumper and drags it onto a trailer bed. The rear bumper squeals and falls off. Melanie shakes Kirk awake. At the corner, surprising the driver very little, they climb down. As the truck pulls away, Kirk tries to hail a cab just letting off a fare.
 A panhandler sees them. "They won' pick you up in this neighborhood."

Kirk throws the VW's bumper in front of the cab and forces it to stop. On the cab's radio, Fats Waller sings:

"ON THE SUNNY SIDE OF THE STREET."

Kirk helps Melanie in and says to the driver, "Sherry North."

"Fare's ten bucks, buddy. You don't look like between you, you got two dimes to rub together."

Melanie leans forward and grimaces. "Listen, camel breath, get this trash heap moving before we twist your chicken neck until your beady little eyes pop out."

Kirk smiles. "Gosh I wish I had that kind of tact. I seldom get past that first difficult conversational opener."

"You develop people skills in my profession." She sits back and engages her most demure look.

The driver turns and probably decides that discretion is truly the better part of valor. When Kirk isn't watching, Melanie tries to take a handful of pills.

He grabs her wrist. "Were any of these prescribed? For you?"

"I don't need a damn prescription."

"Have you seen a doctor about them?"

"I don't need a blood-letter. I told you, I just need—"

He shakes her hand out the window and the pills go flying.

CHAPTER-21
DONUT BASE CAMP

With coffee and donuts filling both hands, Lieutenant Pisanti, Sergeant Moore and Detective Ryan, all pore over ballistics reports and lab photos of Doyle and Maretti. In turn, they all shake their heads.

* * * * * *

At Data Intercept, Ethan holds a file, scans the data: the news photo of Jimmy Doyle's body, the report on the victim in #207, and his report on Jacob Golden. He dials the phone, waits impatiently. "Reservations? I need a seat on your next flight to Buffalo. Open return."

* * * * * *

Kirk pays for a suite at the Sherry North with his platinum card. The desk clerk studiously avoids notice of their colorful attire and unconventional odor. Even their only luggage, Melanie's decanter of Cognac, gets not a second look. Once ensconced in the suite, Melanie heads for the shower while Kirk dials. He gets Ethan's answering machine, dials again, giving Bergdorf-Goodman his and Melanie's sizes. He strips and takes his turn at a shower and uses the complimentary razor. Bergdorf-Goodman arrives with a selection of conservative clothes. With room service promising to deliver their breakfast within ten minutes, they insert the thumb drive into the hotel-supplied computer. Over steaming rich coffee, they view the video.

After a few scratchy, dark, empty seconds of no activity, Melanie, in black, leaves the exhibit area. She enters the closet with the coins. She exits minutes later without them. Moments later, a man enters the closet, emerges with the coins and turns to the camera. It's Smoking Jacket.

* * * * * *

At the drug store, Long Cigar closes his phone. With two bottled waters, they split a handful of aspirin. Hearing Aid inserts his earpiece and turns up the volume. Long Cigar repeats the message: "He's pluggin' into the guy's credit. We're to wait here till he tags their location."

* * * * * *

A seven-foot male secretary, Francis, shows Ethan into Jacob Golden's impressive, studied opulence.

"Thank you, Francis." The giant nods and backs out.

Ethan flips open his notebook. "Just a few questions about your clients, Doyle and Maretti, if you don't mind, sir."

"Who are you? No, never mind. I have no comment."

"Are you aware that both men were shot and killed in little over twenty-four hours?

"Get out of here. Now!"

"I also know that another party was…"

Golden buzzes. Francis enters and escorts/carries Ethan out.

Outside, Ethan waits and watches as Golden leaves his building and heads for the bank of four pay phones on the corner. Only one is unoccupied. Golden makes a short phone call, then returns to his office. Ethan gives the three women at the other phones twenty dollars each and unclips a contact mike and mini-recorder from the fourth phone.

Aboard a Buffalo/New York shuttle flight, Ethan plays back the audio. He listens on earbuds, makes a notation of a phone number. When finished, he dials, repeats the phone number to a phone company supervisor. He gives a coded account number and gets name and address for the phone number.

* * * * * *

Dressed as affluent tourists, Kirk and Melanie view the Havilland Museum's coin collection. Melanie shines a portable UV light on the coins.

Kirk frowns. "You're sure these are not the coins you replaced?"

"You're still treating me like an amateur. I marked all the phony coins to avoid mistakes."

"Maybe they turned them over."

She gives him a disgusted look. "I marked obverse <u>and</u> reverse. Front and back."

"Why would anyone pay to switch counterfeit coins, then put the real coins back?"

"I don't know. We're going ahead with our plan though, right?"

"After a detour."

In their suite, Kirk spreads a large book on the world's rare coins and reads, "Chop mark Brasher Doubloon, unique, owned by the Smithsonian through a generous donation in the 1920's."

With her eyes closed, Melanie is curled against him on the couch. He reads aloud, "The Smithsonian marks all the rare coins in their possession with a laser code. Only the Archivist knows the exact code."

She frowns, "So when the collection got back to D.C. they'd have discovered the fakes."

"That's why they replaced the real coins."

"But then, what good would the fakes be?"

Ethan is admitted and introduced to Melanie Winterhalter. He refuses to talk until she retires to the bedroom. He scribbles something in red on his file cover, gives Kirk the audiotape and the file. "Here's the latest dope." He keeps eyeing the closed bedroom door. Kirk reads the file first, then Ethan's scribbled note. He also looks toward Melanie's door. "Are you sure about this?"

"The facts are correct, Mr. Cannard. You draw your own interpretation of its meaning."

"It's possible the Lieutenant misread those fingernail scratches on the floor of #207."

"What are you saying?"

"He assumed the victim named Marc Voskopf as his killer and he'd just misspelled it 'Mark', then died before he finished the name."

"I don't see what…"

"You might tell the good Lieutenant about that classic Mark V Continental that YOU saw parked in front of my place, license plate 'STYXX.'"

Ethan makes notes and waits.

"When you trace the car, you might also find that the driver smokes cigars…"

"And his prints might match those on the .45…?"

"Right."

"And when exactly did I see this Continental?"

"Why, just before the break-in, naturally."

"What about the other thing?"

"We'll keep that to ourselves for now." He tears the scribbled note into tiny pieces, throws them out the window.

CHAPTER-22
EXPRESS YOURSELF

The Sherry North desk clerk answers the phone, repeats the name, and writes it on a notepad.

"Cannard, Kirk, card number 83118137 0231 1657. Yes, he's a guest, but the charge went through. I already have approval." PAUSE. "Yes, I understand."

He red-flags Kirk's registration slip and dials his room, but gets no answer.

* * * * * * *

Smoking Jacket, comfortable on a blood red velvet settee, takes a sheet from a fax machine, reads and smiles. **Cannard, Kirk—card number 8311 8137 0231 1657—Sherry Netherlands—charges refused—card to be surrendered.**

* * * * * *

Just off the lobby, Kirk studies the hotel's International Room menu. Melanie gives her order directly to the waiter, who seems to consider her explicit instructions an imposition.

"Look, Slick. At these prices, the food better be DAMN good, prepared exactly the way we like, when we like and delivered with PERFECT service."

He looks to Kirk for relief, gets a benign smile in return. Melanie grabs him by his lapel and pulls his head down to her plate.

She whispers loudly. "My boyfriend is a hit man for the FAMILY. Best not to offend him." The waiter looks again to Kirk. Melanie jerks him back to attention. "Wouldn't make eye contact if I were you. Surest way to set him off."

The waiter brings cheesecake for Kirk, sherbet for Melanie. He studiously avoids looking in Kirk's direction.

Long Cigar and Hearing Aid pass the dining room. Spotting Melanie, they change their course and approach. The waiter watches every move in tight-lipped silence. Kirk's hands are in his lap.

Through clenched teeth, Long Cigar says to Kirk, "You don't know us, but..."

"Sure we do. But this is not the place for a conference."

"What I think too."

Hearing Aid adds, "You both oughtta come with us."

"I think not."

Long Cigar reaches under his jacket.

"Don't. You forget you left me your .45 at my place. If you don't want to bleed all over your Montgomery Ward suit, just leave. Maybe I won't turn this gun I'm holding over to the police."

The Maitre d' hands a red-flagged note to the waiter. The waiter watches Long Cigar pull the .32, then recant and with a lot of huffing and puffing, he finally pushes Hearing Aid to the exit.

As Kirk's empty hands reach for Melanie's chair, the waiter tears up the note and their dinner check. To

Kirk, he whispers, "There is no charge. It has been my great pleasure to serve you. Please forgive any error in the service."

Moments later, the doorman holds open the door to the taxi that takes Kirk and Melanie to the Symphony. There's no question that Long Cigar and Hearing Aid are following.

In formal attire, Kirk and Melanie take box seats and look over the crowd. Kirk points out Lieutenant Pisanti in the third row. They don't recognize Smoking Jacket in the seventh row. As the concert begins, Melanie sits forward, obviously captivated by the music.

At intermission, Kirk leans forward while filling Melanie's champagne glass. "You want to tell me?"
"What?"
"You were enraptured by the music. If I'd known it had that effect on you…"
She drops her head as if relating a family scandal. "I wanted to be a concert violinist. It was my major at Boston University."
Surrounded by fans, Marc Voskopf, drawing all attention, enters the foyer.
Kirk looks at her with a new appreciation.
"Why didn't you follow that career?"
"You think everything is just textbook simple? Like in those dumb-ass, self help books you read?"
"Trying is what's important." Cervantes wrote, "The road is better than the inn."
"He wrote that in prison. Your role model was a jailbird."
"So everyone in prison should be dismissed?"

103

"What do you mean?"

"Should we just dismiss everyone in prison?"

"I don't know what you're…"

Lieutenant Pisanti and Ethan, with two young women in tow take the table adjacent to Kirk and Melanie. There is no way to avoid introductions all around.

Kirk asks, "Are you enjoying the music, Lieutenant?"

"Very much so. This young man is tutoring me on the fine points. I'm amazed at his wealth of knowledge."

Ethan blushes slightly. "I'm learning a lot about police procedure."

The two young ladies smile at each other as if they know not to join in the conversation.

Pisanti looks closely at Melanie, "Tell me, Melanie, what is your…?"

The symphony buzzer SOUNDS. Ethan and Kirk simultaneously offer, "Oops, time to take our seats."

Having followed, Long Cigar and Hearing Aid wait patiently outside. With the conclusion of the performance, they diligently search the dissembling crowd. At last they spot their target. "We can't make a move here with so many witnesses."

"Let's follow 'em and find a better spot."

The cab with Kirk and Melanie goes to Central Park. Hearing Aid parks the Continental under a tree and Long Cigar follows on foot to the Central Park Zoo entrance. Hearing Aid hurries after them. In the semidarkness, Long Cigar watches as Kirk pulls Melanie up onto the catwalk overlooking the cages above the lion houses. They're silhouetted against the full moon, but the shot is as impractical as the fiction about Oswald shooting Kennedy.

Unafraid of anything he can't see or hear, Hearing Aid takes the lead. They follow as fast as the darkness will permit. Long Cigar is betrayed by the glow of his stogy and the dim light that flashes on the shiny .32 as he moves slowly.

CHAPTER-23
THEY DON'T PLAY POLO AT NIGHT

At the Polo Grounds, Kirk leads Melanie into a groom's box adjacent a tall black gelding. Moonlight reflects off the brass nameplate over the stall door, "Stardancer, Owner Kirk Cannard."

In soft tones, Kirk explains, "We can't go back to the Sherry. They know we're registered there, so we'll be safe here for the night." In an adjacent empty stall, with his polo mallet at the ready, he throws his tux jacket over her as she cuddles up to him on the fresh straw and is instantly asleep.

Long Cigar and Hearing Aid are separated, lost, and turned around. They finally rejoin near the polo field. As a last resort, they check the stables. Long Cigar sees Kirk's name over the stall. They both look into the dark stall. With his good hand, he reaches into Stardancer's stall. Hearing Aid YEOWLS in pain and tries to shake a round body from his ankle. The startled horse kicks at the sound, catches Long Cigar's good hand on the latch. He HOWLS, drops the .32 into a pile of straw.

Kirk hears the two men stumble off in the darkness, bumping into objects as they go. Melanie smiles in her undisturbed sleep.

* * * * * *

At Police Headquarters, Lieutenant Pisanti and Ethan—both still in tuxes--check the DMV record of Continental owners. Out of Ethan's hearing, an on-duty cop asks, "What's the deal, Lou? You adopt the kid?"

"He's all right. Has his own agenda. I don't know what, but as long as I keep him close and he continues feeding me information, I won't rock the boat."

* * * * * *

Long Cigar holds his broken hand under the same E.R. vet's red-rimmed eyes. Hearing Aid hops on one foot; holds his other bleeding ankle. Hanging from it is a small but determined box turtle.

* * * * * *

Just after dawn, at the Tavern On The Green, Kirk answers his beeper as Melanie orders OJ, oatmeal and black coffee for two. The waiter brings a wireless house phone to the table, discreetly averts his eyes from the straw in Melanie's hair and Kirk's wrinkled tux.

Ethan's voice comes filtered through phone lines. "Trouble. Somebody's canceled your credit."

"Are you sure?"

"Sir, I run hundreds of credit checks a month."

Melanie overhears, fingers her platinum necklace as he hangs up.

"There's a pawnshop on 47th. We can get enough for a few days at least."

Kirk gently takes her hand down and seems reluctant to let go. "Thanks, but it's not time to panic. Yet."

He dials again. "This is Kirk Cannard. I understand there's some misunderstanding about my hotel bill. You might check with Mr. Krump." PAUSE. "Oh, he's already taken care of it? Well, thank you. Yes, we wish to keep the suite." To the question on Melanie's face, he responds with, "The hotel owner plays polo."

Back in their Sherry North suite, wearing expensive conservative tweeds, Kirk plays Ethan's mini-recorder.

Golden's voice is nervous, but Smoking Jacket is calm. Their filtered voices are clear.

> Golden-There's a problem. Some nosey kid was here asking embarrassing questions about Doyle.

Melanie adds, "That's Jacob Golden, the weasel. I never should have trusted him."

> Smoking Jacket-You were to get me somebody clean. You brought in a has-been.

Melanie adds, "The other voice must be the one behind all this, the pig."

> Golden-Unimportant now. You cut the girl out. She still owes me the seven-hundred-thousand she expected from you.
> Smoking Jacket-I'll pay. There's no reason to involve her.
> Golden-But she IS involved. I wouldn't be surprised if she's caused all these problems.
> Smoking Jacket-I'll handle it.
> Golden-You're not going to...
> Smoking Jacket-I'll do what has to be done.

Golden-Whatever it is, I don't want to know.

With clenched fists, Melanie jumps to her feet. "The other one must be the one in the video, the sneak who took my coins. And DePalma had the thumb drive so he's obviously in on it."

Kirk pulls her down onto the couch. "His name is Sullivan and he lives aboard the sloop "Styxx", not far from my boat."

"It's called a ship, or a vessel."

"Right. Anyway, he probably has the coins aboard. I figure DePalma made the tape so he didn't wind up on a stainless steel table like the others."

"We still don't know Sullivan's plans."

"I'd assume he's selling fake coins. His cover would be that he has the real coins and the museum has the fakes. That's why Doyle had to be captured on the scene. The news had to get out that the museum security had been broken and the coins had been out of their possession even for a few moments."

"And the museum recovered the real coins, because in the interval, Sullivan had them switched back."

"And since the real coins were put back, they'll pass the laser test, but that information wouldn't be passed to the public. Now! I think you have some BACK STORY to tell me. Something about your father?"

"How…? Okay, I guess you deserve the truth. He was sentenced to Dannamorra for ten years. You probably know for what."

"Cat burglary. Cartier's lost seven million in uncut stones. They were never recovered. I remember the news story."

"Anyway, prison life is hard on him. Golden said he'd get him out for a million dollars. I gave him my two-hundred-thousand savings."

"Plus the hundred-fifty-thousand and the balance due from Sullivan. Why not let Dad use some of the loot from the Cartier job?"

He gets an incredulous look from Melanie. "That's his retirement fund. Anyway, it's all blown now. How did you find out?"

"Ethan. And Winterhalter isn't a common name in prison." PAUSE. "Were you going to tell me?"

"Truthfully? No. There was no reason to. Two weeks after I'm gone you'll even forget my name."

Kirk looks away and thinks, *Maybe...not.*

From an adjacent suite, Fats Waller sings:

"I'VE GOT A FEELING I'M FALLING."

* * * * * *

A Lear jet arrives at the Executive Terminal. The Smithsonian man in dark grey suit with matching umbrella steps down and is greeted by DePalma, who gets only a tight-lipped nod on the way to the museum limo.

CHAPTER-24
SAM SPADE HAD TO DO HIS OWN LEG WORK

In Ethan's office, Kirk reads the screen over Ethan's shoulder as it scrolls past Data Intercept material already surveyed. He has Ethan copy a back up of the part about the Smithsonian representative arriving. He pulls Melanie over to read the screen. "The coins are going back today."

She points to the screen data. "What's this?"

Ethan explains. "Many corporations donate private-jet time to nonprofit organizations like the Smithsonian. They take it as a tax loss."

She grins at Kirk. "Does that mean what I think?"

"We'll act on the assumption that it does. We need to get Lieutenant Pisanti on it. Ethan, take a hard copy and get your NYPD friend to stop this plane before it takes off for Washington."

She dials and calls Kirk to the phone.

"Mr. Sullivan, Kirk Cannard. I'm a collector of various items and I've decided to expand my interests. It's recently come to my attention that you are in possession of several VERY desirable coins." PAUSE. "No, I trust my sources. It's either sell to me or explain to Lieutenant Pisanti your noninvolvement in two deaths, several other attempts, a museum heist, several apartment break-ins and...." PAUSE. "Yes, I thought you'd see it my way." PAUSE. "I'll be there in twenty minutes." PAUSE. "Yes, I know where." PAUSE. "No! There's no reason for her to come."

Melanie pulls the phone from his hand. "You bet your ass I'll be there."

Kirk tries to grab the phone back, but she hangs up

"Let's go. You said twenty minutes."

She takes the brandy decanter and heads for the door.

* * * * * *

Golden and DePalma stand in a dark corner of the taped-off hallway. They watch silently as the Smithsonian Man supervises armed guards loading the coin exhibit into the armored truck.

DePalma whispers. "I told you, the cash would be delivered to me at the airport. You'll get your cut then."

"But I can't wait around. I've an established practice to get back to."

"If you're smart, you'll do as I'm doing. I'm escorting this clown to D.C., then taking my five million to the Bahamas."

"You're not coming back?"

"For a lousy taxed fifty-thousand a year?"

"But your reputation? Well, maybe you're right. I'll ride with you to D.C. and make a decision on the way."

* * * * * *

Lieutenant Pisanti and Ethan descend the police station steps three at a time, climb into a police car and pull away, with red lights and SIREN.

* * * * * *

Spreading a huge suitcase filled with five million in cash atop his French Provincial mahogany desk, Smoking Jacket motions Hearing Aid to take it. He gives Long Cigar a new attaché case with a hidden compartment. Inside is a .44 magnum. To Long Cigar he says, "Once you deliver the money, I don't want Golden or DePalma to leave the plane alive."

"We can dump the bodies in the Atlantic, but we'll have to go along and take out the pilot too, after we land at D.C."

"All in the line of duty. Use some of the cash to fly back first class. I'll give you your bonuses out of the remaining amount."

Long Cigar tries to pick up the case with both hands bandaged.

Finally Hearing Aid limps over and picks it up. "I'll get it. You'd probly lose it or shoot yourself in the foot. You don't have a good record with guns lately."

Long Cigar punches him with his bandaged fist, grimaces in pain, and the two leave.

* * * * * *

Along the apron of the road, the speeding black and white passes traffic all the way to the airport. Lieutenant Pisanti and Ethan reach peak anticipation.

"Tell me, kid, do you wear red suspenders and bow tie to bed, too?"

"Nope. There and in the shower's the only two places, though."

"Some religious fetish or something, huh?"

"Close. As a young girl, my mother had a mad crush on Van Johnson. She sent him love letters. He sent her a pair of his sox that he'd worn in some motion picture."

"Let me guess. Red sox?"

"Only kind he ever wore. It started as a joke. My dad and I have always understood. It's something we'd grown to accept."

"I still don't see why…"

"Red sox is weird. So I decided to add the red tie and suspenders."

"For how long?"

"I never stipulated."

"I guess it makes your mom happy."

"It did. She died three years ago."

CHAPTER-25
EXECUTIVE TERMINALS ARE MORE PLEASANT

On the tarmac, DePalma and Golden wait anxiously aboard the Lear jet for the delivery of the money. The Continental arrives, but is held behind the gate. Hearing Aid pulls into one of the "Owner" parking slots. Long Cigar reaches for the attaché case. They see the police car pull to the plane and watch Lieutenant Pisanti take Golden and DePalma into custody. Hearing Aid pulls the Continental into a tight turn.

The Smithsonian Man and Lieutenant Pisanti engage in some kind of gesticulating, verbal dispute. The Smithsonian Man uses a briefcase scramble phone to call someone. Lieutenant Pisanti awaits the results.

* * * * * *

Kirk and Melanie board "Styxx" and are shown into the main salon by a uniformed deck hand. Melanie pours from her cut-glass decanter into glasses on a sideboard. Unseen by Smoking Jacket, she empties the contents of the owl's tranquilizer into one glass and hands it to Smoking Jacket. She and Kirk drink theirs as a toast. Smoking Jacket holds his. Kirk looks around with an appraising eye. "Very nice. What's top speed?"

Melanie refills her glass. "Never mind that. What's the main stateroom like?"

"Also, we're interested in what you did with the coins?"

"I haven't the foggiest notion what you are talking about. Some kind of illegal activity?"

"Skip it. We know all about the heist, the break-ins, the killings."

"What she means to say is, we want a 25% cut of the coin deal."

Smoking Jacket glances to the portrait of a ship captain. Melanie follows his eyes.

"Who's that? Morgan the pirate? Must be a relative."

Kirk goes to the portrait, lifts it away, and exposes a large safe door. Smoking Jacket nervously downs his brandy.

Screeching tires announce the Continental's return. Hearing Aid crowds inside, and at the sight of Melanie, Long Cigar drops the money and pulls the .44 from the attaché case.

Kirk smiles. "I see you escaped. Fear of flying, perhaps."

Melanie shakes her head, "Must be too dumb to have gone aboard." To Smoking Jacket she says, "You obviously didn't intend them to avoid the bomb."

"Whatever are you talking about?"

"Come off it. Sullivan Enterprises Ltd. owns the plane. No baggage checks."

Kirk adds, "The course is over water. No embarrassing wreckage to sift through."

Melanie empties her glass. "You wanted the world to know the coins were out of custody for a short time, then led Doyle into a trap to quell an immediate investigation."

"We sent the police to stop the flight. Figured you'd have planted a bomb aboard somehow."

Melanie pours another double brandy into Kirk's glass. "No, two makes me…" She looks him off! He realizes her intent and downs the double.

Long Cigar looks from one to the other, confused, turns back to Smoking Jacket. "Cops showed up. It's why we came back. Din't know nothin' 'bout a bomb."

Melanie stares at the two dupes. "He had fakes ready to supply to collectors willing to buy stolen coins they could never display. He would destroy the real coins and cut his partners out at the same time, all with one bomb. Look in the case."

Hearing Aid, trying to follow the action says, "What?"

Melanie moves to his side, turns his hearing Aid up full volume, YELLS at him. "He says give him the gun, dummy."

Hearing Aid recoils from her. Kirk twists the .44 from Long Cigar's hand and shoves him into Smoking Jacket. Melanie pulls the lit cigar from his mouth as he passes. She aims it at Smoking Jacket's eye. She misses, but puts a serious burn in his cheek.

Kirk and Melanie jump ashore. They pull the restraining ropes and push the craft away from the dock. Long Cigar and Hearing Aid stumble to the rail. They jump, but miss the dock. Hearing Aid grabs the edge, catches Long Cigar as he's about to drop into the water. Melanie, with a pawl wrench is about to smash Hearing Aid's hand. Kirk stops her, slips a loop of rope over Long Cigar's head and shoulders, pulls them both up, but keeps the rope on.

Melanie looks daggers at the two killers. "Give me the gun."

"You can't kill them."

"Yes, I can."

"No you can't!"

"Why not?"

"It's against yacht club rules."

"Sharks would get them. Either that or the tide would take them into the harbor. Either way, nobody'd know they came from here."

"Still, it's not sporting."

"I'll go to confession, say three Hail Marys' and leave a twenty in the poor box."

In the background, police SIRENS blare.

"We can't get involved and the police'll be here any minute."

"Well, we can't just leave them. What if I just break both their knee caps?"

"You don't really want to do that."

"Yes, I do!"

"My way or the highway."

"Damn. You're taking all the fun out of this." She loops one shank of rope around Long Cigar's ankle and another around Hearing Aid's, ties them through the chain holding a huge weather balloon high above their heads, then resets the cog in the ratchet, so when she releases the pawl, the balloon soars twenty feet higher into the air, taking Long Cigar and Hearing Aid, both hanging upside-down, with it.

"Styxx" drifts lazily into a coast guard vessel. Smoking Jacket is slumped on the floor, sleeping from the vet's tranquilizer. He's beside the open safe. Lacking dexterity, he tried vainly to save trays of fake Brasher Doubloons.

Ethan and the police arrive. Lieutenant Pisanti takes Long Cigar and Hearing Aid into custody.

CHAPTER-26
OVERLOOKING CENTRAL PARK

On the balcony, Kirk and Melanie, in a pair of silk PJ's—he the bottoms, she the tops—enjoy chilled grapefruit and black coffee.

She shakes her head. "I'm not tying up with anybody whose source of income is so hazy."

"Not hazy at all. I sold a patent for structured escherichia coli."

"Structured e...?"

"It's a hyper-bacteria that digests waste vegetation and converts it into methane."

"They've had that for years. My dad told me that Germany ran the war on methane fuel for their trucks."

"Yes, but my process is simple, economical and portable. In one week Central Park could power all the city vehicles for a month. A consortium of the major petroleum companies paid me truckloads of money for distribution rights and..."

"You sold out. They'll bury it."

"...AND they have five years, then it becomes public domain."

Lucinda brings fresh coffee and refills their cups. "We outta cat food. Kiva mus' be feedin' a litter." She returns to the kitchen.

"All I can guarantee at this point is enough work on crystal regulators, Morbiers, Swingers, inclined plains, astrologicals, French silk thread..."

"I didn't know you knew so much about clocks."

"I've recently been studying."

The sound of...

"AIN'T MISBEHAVIN'"

announces a visitor. Melanie checks the closed circuit. "Let them in, please? No, wait. Let me get dressed first."

"Why the sudden modesty?"

"PLEASE!"

Kirk opens and admits Lieutenant Pisanti and Ethan. Melanie is back in record time, dressed in conservative silk blouse and leather skirt. She maintains an innocent air that works, if you don't notice that the buttons on her blouse are misholed. They all do, but say nothing.

Lieutenant Pisanti takes the offered coffee and says, "Jacob Golden has turned states' evidence. He's given us the whole coin-hoist story. He's also involved you and your father, Miss Winterhalter."

"There's no proof that—"

"I expected you'd have an answer, Mr. Cannard. Let me clarify my position before anyone says something that's impossible to retract."

"The Smithsonian wants no hint that such fakes could be made. They fear others might be more successful. Not these, but numismatic coins in the $500.00 to $5,000.00 range."

Kirk pours himself a double brandy. "So, Lieutenant, you want our help in downplaying that part of the story?"

"In a way, yes. The two who committed the murders knew nothing of the coins or the reason for the hits. They'll plead to second degree, along with Sullivan, in exchange for their silence."

Melanie looks about ready to explode. "What about their attempt on my life and...?"

Kirk interrupts her with, "Not worth waking sleeping giants." To Pisanti, "What about DePalma?"

"He resigned, and the museum doesn't want to make waves. The problem comes from Golden, and how to defuse him."

Kirk frowns. "I'm curious as to just what needs to be defused. In other words, what story did he conjure?"

Melanie jumps between the two. "Whatever it was, it's a lie."

"He says he contracted with Sullivan to supply a cat burglar and a fence."

"Well, he did. Doyle and Maretti."

"He admits that, but claims he also sent Miss Winterhalter. Said he'd had prior dealings with her and that she'd learned her trade from her father."

"Why would Miss Winterhalter agree to such a thing? She has a promising career of her own."

"That's all it would take to close the case. I'm here for damage control. If I can convince my superiors that Miss Winterhalter is innocent, well, Golden has no proof and he'll get ten years anyway."

From the radio, Fats Waller sings:

"NOBODY WANTS YOU WHEN YOU'RE DOWN AND OUT."

Melanie looks defeated. "I might as well admit…"

Kirk jumps in with, "That she has signed a contract with The Atlantic Pops as guest soloist." He dials downstairs. "Marc, maybe you'd explain to Lieutenant Pisanti about Miss Winterhalter practicing with you for her debut with the Atlantic Pops." PAUSE. "Great, we'll be right down."

Melanie shakes her head. "I can't…"

"Sure you can. The Lieutenant realizes you've not practiced, with all that's happened, and you may be a bit rusty. I'm sure he'll take that into account."

CHAPTER-27
MUSIC APPRECIATION

Marc admits Kirk and Melanie, Lieutenant Pisanti and Ethan. All take seats on the divan and look to the dais. Kirk speaks quietly to Marc. Melanie stands behind him, in almost paralyzing shock. Marc hands her a violin, she tunes it to his piano, takes a deep breath and tries to think of a selection. Marc, at the piano, waits for her choice. He has Braille music before him.

Selecting from a stack of sheet music, Kirk sets it on the stand in front of her. "This is one of my favorites, the scherzo from Mendelssohn's Midsummer Night's Dream."

Marc smiles. "A lovely piece. He wrote it when he was only seventeen."

Melanie reads the music, follows Marc's lead. After a few bars something goes wrong. Marc follows, with general chords at a stumbling pace. Melanie doesn't know why everyone but Lieutenant Pisanti is looking at her strangely.

Ethan whispers to Kirk, "Why is she playing it backward?"

"Ssh. I'll explain it when you're a little older."

Lieutenant Pisanti applauds. "That was fine, but could you play something I might recognize?"

Melanie controls her temporary stress, "How's this?" From memory she plays.

"THE GARRYOWEN."

She's good. Not soloist material, but such a judgment is beyond the Lieutenant.

CHAPTER-28
PARKS AREN'T JUST FOR KIDS AND DOGS

At the Polo Grounds, three weeks later, Kirk's team finishes with a winning score. He canters across the field to where Melanie sits cheering. She hands him a face towel. Still in the saddle, he spots Lieutenant Pisanti, Ethan and an older man, working their way through the crowd toward the rail.

Melanie looks up into Kirk's eyes. "Kirk, I'd like you to meet my father, Douglas." She hugs her father who gives her a beaming smile.

From tall in the saddle, he leans down and shakes the man's hand, then turns to Lieutenant Pisanti. "Well, Lieutenant, to what do we owe this favor?"

"There's nothing wrong with my imagination, but around you two, I seem not to need it. We figure you deserve to be altogether when we give you the news."

Melanie stands and says, "I'm afraid, Lieutenant, you have us at—"

"It's Captain. I solved two murders in less than a week, thanks to you two."

Melanie looks questioningly at her father, says nothing.

"The good Captain thinks he can swing an early release for my testimony against Golden."

"I need no embellishment of the truth."

"To what do you refer, Captain?"

"Like, if I were to ask you both for alibis for the time of the coin theft, I'd have to expect an answer."

Kirk leads Stardancer to the stables and unsaddles the proud equine. The others follow.

"My boat is docked at the Fair Winds Yacht Club. On that night, we…"

Lieutenant Pisanti interrupts. "I'm not asking. I feel it best to close the case without making more waves."

Kirk, to Douglas, "You were offered a lighter sentence if you'd return the stones?"

"I've already spent three years behind bars. I was facing only another three with good behavior. It seemed a poor bargain."

Ethan, in the temporary silence, adds, "I've been made New York Times crime investigative reporter. All due to a story that I can't publish."

A groom takes the horse to be washed and brushed.

"Based on your suggestions, Mr. Winterhalter, Golden has donated three-hundred-fifty-thousand dollars to the New York Zoological Society."

Ethan adds, "And DePalma contributed seven-hundred-thousand to the Police Widow and Orphan Fund."

Melanie, with eyes blazing, stamps her foot, "That's my mon…"

Kirk squeezes her hand. She grudgingly clamps her mouth shut.

"Real money, not counterfeit like what he sent to pay off DePalma and Golden."

"Well, he planned for the plane to go down in the briny deep, leaving no witnesses. There was no need to lose real cash."

Douglas shows the handcuffs he's wearing, "I may be out in less than a year."

They all turn to Lieutenant Pisanti. The plane and pilot were both heavily insured. With Sullivan Enterprises as beneficiary, he'd even have come out ahead on that score. We traced his forger who did the currency. He's the same one did the coins."

Melanie, with her best airhead impression, "What coins exactly are those, Captain? You never did give us any facts."

Kirk postulates, "I think it's something to do with overthrowing some third world country."

Lieutenant Pisanti looks at them both, answers slowly. "Something like that. As I said, I can't divulge any details. National security. You understand. I'm grateful for the tickets, Mr. Cannard. I've become quite a polo fan. Turning to Melanie. I've also taken an interest in classical music. I'd planned to attend all Atlantic Pops similar functions. I was saddened to see you were not listed as soloist, Miss Winterhalter."

From a radio somewhere in the stable, Fats Waller sings:

"HONEYSUCKLE ROSE."

Kirk holds up her left hand. A seven-karat ring sparkles from her third finger. "She's decided to give up all commercial ventures. We'll be sailing to Nice and the Riviera next month for our honeymoon."

She gives Kirk a sweet smile, but says to Lieutenant Pisanti, "Naturally, I'll keep my talents honed, but just as a hobby, of course."

As the others leave and he's holding her tightly and lifting her chin for a kiss, she says in a soft, hypnotic voice, "I guess it's a good thing you didn't know that you had me at, *'I'll have to teach you to swim if you insist on these water sports'.*"

AFTERWARD

Proof reading and rewriting as many times as it takes is like restoring an abandoned and abused Duesenberg. You don't want to show it before you've removed any rust, replaced broken parts and dressed her in new paint.

INTRODUCTION TO E-BOOKS

Please allow me to share the following E books with you. Order all from Amazon.com and remember, positive word of mouth is the best form of advertisement.

13-An Hour's Pleasure
16-A Taste of Money
19-A Torch Unseen
21-Black Kat
12-Cold Fire
7-Fantasy Impromptu
3-Fools Rush In
6-Greene's Field
9-Houston, We Have A Problem
2-Independence
17-Just For Kids
4-Just Passin' Thru
1-Liberty
11-Naked We Came
8-Nature Abhors a Vacuum
22-Night Train and Country Gravy
18-One Fist is Iron
20-September 17th
10-Shallow Water
14-The Angel and The Eighteen Wheeler
23-The Big E
15-'37 Indian
5-Writer's Block

ALL my E-books is good. Some is even GOODER.

EXCERPT JUST PASSIN' THRU   7-15-14

CHAPTER-1
MAMMA TOLD YOU NOT TO PICK UP HITCH-HIKERS

On highway #55, south of Jackson, Mississippi, a primer-painted pickup truck shows in the distance, then disappears. On the corrugated road, it alternately dips out of sight, then appears again as it advances. Just ahead is a Mississippi highway 20-E road sign with an arrow pointing right. Beside the signpost are two expensive glove leather suitcases and Tracy, a very attractive young woman in high heels and short cocktail dress. As the truck approaches, she holds out her thumb in the traditional hitchhiker's pose.

The truck's radio plays:

THERE'S A PLACE FOR US.

As the truck pulls to a dusty stop, Scott, thirtyish with rugged good looks, leans over and pushes open the passenger door. Tracy gives the truck a jaundiced look. Even the California license plate is mud-caked. "Huh, just my luck. A pickup. Could as easily have been a limo with some rich oil baron."

Not looking as apologetic as his words might suggest, "Sorry, only oil I got's on a rag under the seat. I'm just passin' through your state."

"Ugh! Mississippi is not my state. I want as far from here as I can be."

"Where you headed?"
"Memphis, I guess."
"Is Memphis on the way to Chattanooga?"
"Not unless you're seriously lost."
"What about highway 20? Is that a good way?"
"Only if you want to take a month getting there."
She lifts her cases into the truck bed and, before climbing into the cab, wipes the seat with a lace handkerchief. She stares at the filthy handkerchief and, with an act of total rejection, throws it out the window.
"Just drop me at a bus depot. I'll make it from there."

For a half-hour they drive in silence. Both seem somewhere else and lost in thought. When he finds the Jackson bus depot, he lets her off.
"Thanks...?"
"Scott."
"Thanks, Scott. I'm Tracy. 'Bye."
He turns onto highway 20-E, but correcting, regains 55-N. Just over the rise, the pickup coughs, bucks and dies. Coasting down the gradual decline, Scott pulls to a store's single gas pump. "Top it off and sell me an inline gas filter. I'll put it in myself. Tank's taken on some water."
The mechanic/owner sees the California plates and a spotless engine compartment, twin four-barrel carbs atop a sparkling new engine. With a full tank, the new filter in place, Scott pays with a century note. The mechanic/owner counts out $7.37 change and notes the empty wallet. He watches as Scott tries without any luck, to start the truck.
"Can you give me a jump?"
With a shake of his head, the Mechanic/owner, says, "You need the tank drained and the lines blown out. I

could do it for two hundred plus parts. But you might also need new carburetors."

"You're kidding, right? This is a factory-rebuilt 426 Hemi, with less than three thousand miles."

"'Course, you might have ignition problems too. We can't tell that 'til we clean the fuel system."

"Look, I'm not some fat, dumb, rich tourist."

"You sayin' I'm tryin' ta take advantage of ya?"

"What? No. Never. I'm not lookin' for trouble, just tryin' to get home,. I'm only goin' another couple hundred miles."

"If ya don't have the money right now, you could leave it. Fifty bucks a day storage. Or I could tow ya someplace. Ony twelve bucks a mile."

With a sigh, Scott says, "You interested in buying a truck?"

"Might be, at five hundred bucks."

"It's worth over twenty five thousand in California. The engine alone is worth twenty by itself. Give me that much and it's yours."

"You ain't in California. I'll give ya two hundred fifty bucks. In another five minutes, it'll be one twenty-five. After that, storage'll be ten bucks an hour."

"Yeah, thanks. Real hospitable state." He pushes the truck out onto the highway. Seventy yards downhill from the station, it coasts to a stop. He uses starter fluid and grinds away until the battery quits. The mechanic watches, shakes his head and returns to the store.

The Jackson Bus Depot is hectic. With regular employees on strike, scab drivers try to cope with schedules, routes and company policies. Tracy takes a seat in the Memphis bus. The woman across the aisle leans over.

"We was supposed to be on the road a hour ago. This strike thing is got everything messed up."

"Tell me about it. I should have eaten when I had the chance. Now, I just want to take off my shoes and sleep."

"Them's right pretty clothes. You a actress or somebody else important?"

"'Fraid not, just..."

The driver climbs aboard and shouts, "Memphis. All aboard for Memphis."

Those already on board, grumble. The bus crosses the picket line and moves onto the highway.

Tracy fans herself. "Doesn't the air conditioner work?"

"Oh, I reckon they'll get it fixed, soon's cold weather comes. Same time the heater gives out."

Back on the highway, Scott pulls the CD deck from the dash and shoves it into his duffle bag. Pushing an oily rag into the gas tank, he soaks up gasoline and holds a match to the rag. Lifting his western saddle and duffle bag from the bed. As the truck billows a black oily flame, the mechanic, with his jaw hanging open, comes out to stare. Without looking back, Scott walks off down the center of the highway.

CHAPTER-2
AN ACQUAINTANCE REUNITED

The bus passes a store/gas station and then detours around a burning hulk. Only minutes later, it stops for the waving pedestrian in the middle of the road. Scott boards, stacks his saddle atop the duffle bag. The only empty seat is by a window past a woman in a short cocktail dress rubbing her feet. He fails at first to recognize Tracy.

"'Scuze me, ma'am, can I sit...? Oh, hello."

"What are you doing here? This isn't the way to Chattanooga."

"I got lost right after I let you off."

She gives him a look that says she expected no less. Not long later, the bus is overtaken and stopped by red lights and...

SIREN.

A Mississippi sheriff climbs aboard. With a hand on his gun, he gives Scott a lopsided grin. "Come on, son. We don't cotton to folks settin' fire to they own truck and leavin' it burnin' to a crisp 'side the road. Messes our scenic beauty."

Tracy puts out her arm, blocking Scott. "You're overstepping yourself, Sheriff. Unless you were an eyewitness, you have merely an alleged crime. And if your only evidence is burned beyond recognition, you've no proof even of ownership. State code #42 says you can't even ask for I.D."

"But..."

"In any event, you have no jurisdiction over an interstate public carrier on a U.S. highway. You get a warrant and I'll surrender my client in proper legal fashion."

The sheriff backs off; scratches his head, and the bus drives off.

With an appreciative look, Scott says, "Thanks, I'd never have taken you for a lawyer."

"I'm not, but I worked for one in New Orleans. I'm just repaying a favor. But if I were you, I'd get off at the next stop. What these redneck sheriffs lack in brains they make up for in tenacity."

"I'll never get home if I do that."
"Suit yourself."

A few miles later, the bus is putting miles below it when a, long, low, black convertible pulls in front and...

HONKS.

It, slows, forcing the bus to stop behind it. Tracy can't see anything happening outside. "What kind of car is that is?"
"It's a Stuz Blackhawk. I've seen a few around Hollywood."
"Oh no, Bobbie. Not again."
"Who is it? Your boyfriend or husband?"
"He's trying to be either, or both."
"It's not a mutual attraction?"
"I loathe and despise everything about him."

Bobbie climbs aboard. Tracy shrinks low in her seat, but he spots her. Scott moves into the aisle and pushes the man aside. "'Scuze me, cousin, reckon I'll get out and stretch my legs."
"Tracy, you stop this nonsense. Come off this foul thing."
"Go away, Bobbie. Don't follow me, don't call, don't write, don't even think about me."
"Come on." With a dismissive hand gesture he indicates the rest of the passengers. "You don't belong with people like these."
Scott reboards, nudges the man roughly aside and reclaims his seat. "That's some fancy car, mister. But you musta hit some sharp rocks. They flattened two tires on ya."

138

"What?" Bobbie rushes up the aisle. As he steps off, a front passenger levers the door shut and the driver needs no urging. Leaving dust and a sooty black cloud, he pulls back onto the highway, throwing gravel onto the kneeling Bobbie.

> That's it. If I gave you any more, you wouldn't have to buy the book. *Vaughn*

www.ingramcontent.com/pod-product-compliance
Lightning Source LLC
Chambersburg PA
CBHW060017050426
42448CB00012B/2790